# JOURNEY

# BI

## John Drane

SCRIPTURE UNION

Scripture Union, 207–209 Queensway, Bletchley, MK2 2EB,
England.
Email: info@scriptureunion.org.uk
Web site: www.scriptureunion.org.uk

ISBN 1 85999 409 1

Except where otherwise stated, Scriptures are quoted from the
*Good News Bible* published by the Bible Societies/HarperCollins
Publishers Limited, UK American Bible Society, 1966, 1971, 1976,
1992.

British Library Cataloguing-in-Publication Data
A catalogue record for this book is available from the British Library.

Cover design by ie design
Printed and bound in Great Britain by Creative Print and Design
(Wales) Ebbw Vale.

# Contents

# Preface

This book had its origins in the mid-1980s, and it was a surprise when Andrew Clark, editor with Scripture Union Publishing, invited me to revise and update it for a fresh edition that would meet the needs of Bible readers in the new century. Widespread changes have taken place in our culture in the course of the last fifteen years, and many of the questions we now wrestle with were unheard of then. Not surprisingly, I spent some time trying to decide exactly how to revise this material in a way that would make it most accessible to today's readers. In the end, I went back to its original purpose, which was not to address those who were already knowledgeable about the Bible, but rather to help those who might be struggling to come to terms with it for the first time – whether young people, or those who have recently come to faith.

It is easy enough to agree that for Christians the Bible should be a vital component in an effective spirituality. Yet when we actually try to come to grips with it, it can often seem to be a very difficult book indeed, written by people from a different time and place to address matters that, however important they may have been then, are simply not part of today's agenda. What is in here is unlikely to be the final word for those who are engaged in a long-term search to uncover what the Bible might be saying to them today. But if it even begins to help identify some useful questions, and opens up new possibilities through which God can speak to our everyday circumstances, it will have achieved its aim.

*John Drane, King's College, Aberdeen*

*Chapter 1*

# Checking out the territory

The cheerfu' supper done, wi' serious face
They, round the ingle, form a circle wide;
The sire turns o'er, wi' patriarchal grace,
The big ha'-Bible, ance his father's pride...
He wales a portion with judicious care,
And 'Let us worship God!' he says, with solemn air.

That was how Robert Burns described the high point of the evening in his celebrated poem, 'The Cotter's Saturday Night'. It so happens that Burns was at home in eighteenth-century Scotland. But the time and place could be anywhere. For the picture he so deftly paints, of a good parent sharing the Word of God with the children, still tugs the heart strings of many people today.

Two and a half centuries ago, the French philosopher Voltaire claimed, 'Another century and there will not be a Bible on earth.' Yet here we are today, in a world that has changed beyond recognition, and the Bible is still the best-selling book of all time, translated into more languages than any other, and to be found in the majority of homes in the developed world. Of course, that does not mean that the Bible is read by those who possess a copy. The steep decline of the church, particularly in Europe, over the last twenty years or so almost certainly means that fewer people than ever before in the Western world ever open its pages. But the fact that the Bible's essential values are deeply rooted in our culture has ensured that it is still generally held in high regard, and even those who would never dream of having any regular involvement in the life of the church nevertheless find in this remarkable book an inspirational quality that is hard to locate elsewhere. Paul's great poem in praise of love (1 Corinthians 13) has made its own mark as a masterpiece of world literature – while the principles taught by Jesus have come to form the basis of what we understand by civilized behaviour.

Even in today's world, there are those who still try to model their lives on what they see as the simple faith of the Bible. The home-spun lifestyle of the Amish and Mennonite communities scattered around North America would not suit most of us – and yet they have become major tourist attractions, as if those who are puzzled by the complexity of life have a secret admiration for people who seem to have peace of mind and a settled faith. There was a time when most Christians lived like this, at least so far as Bible reading is concerned. In many families the day couldn't start – or end – properly without prayer and Bible reading. Even if we didn't always quite make it, the scene depicted in Robert Burn's poem was something that most Christians would have aspired to in the past. There are probably a few families and individuals still like that today, but for most it is a very different story. Even committed Christians rarely live that way. They may come to the start of a new year with firm and serious resolutions that regular Bible study must feature in their lives for the following twelve months, but by the end of February their best intentions are beginning to tail off, and by the time Easter comes around they have all but given up – with the Bible only occasionally slotted into the daily schedule to help ease a guilty conscience.

I remember once being in a church building that was about to be redecorated. At the Sunday services, the minister appealed to those people who left their Bibles in the pews from one Sunday to the next to take them away for just one week, so they would not be splashed with paint. After the service, Bibles that had never seen the inside of a house for years were gathered up by the armful! I don't know whether that meant they were read at home that week, but I guess not. No doubt there were many reasons why those particular people always left their Bibles behind in church, not necessarily related to the level of their faith or commitment. On the whole, today's Christians are no less committed than those of previous generations – in fact, with the general decline of churchgoing today, those of us who are still left are probably even more dedicated, because it takes a certain tenacity and determination to go against the flow of our culture. But that doesn't mean we have no struggles. In the context of the kind of hectic lifestyles that we all now have, we tend to look for things with immediate results – and, on that score, Bible reading often seems to come out quite badly.

No doubt that is why so many Christians find themselves locked into a syndrome of despair about personal habits of Bible reading and study. Every now and again we feel impelled to make new promises – to ourselves, to our friends, and to God – only to find we soon end up on the old familiar slippery slope to gradual failure. Until the next time, that is – and in the meantime we may feel guilty, lazy, or just plain inadequate as Christians. Most Christians will have been here a few times, at least. I certainly have, and it's worth observing here that sustained Bible reading is often no less problematical for Christian leaders and ministers than it is for others. An even bigger challenge for most is how to read the Bible in a helpful and positive way with others who share the same home.

Stating the problem is the easy part: knowing how to tackle it is going to be more difficult. First let me repeat something I have already said. I do not believe modern Christians are, on the whole, any less committed than previous generations have been. Nor do I think any of us need lose heart. Above all, never imagine that everyone in your church except you knows all about Bible reading and does it much more successfully. Believe me, they don't, and if people claim in meetings that they have never had a problem they're almost certainly bluffing. The fact is that the vast majority of Christians have good intentions all along the line. We want to know our faith better. We want to get closer to God through reading the Scriptures. We want the Bible to be a light along the way, and a guide throughout life, and all those other grand things that preachers tell us it is supposed to be. But the bottom line is that we are generally at a loss to know how to read and apply it to our own everyday lives. Of course, in a general sort of way we expect God to speak to us through this book. But it's often a different story as we plough laboriously through Genesis, or Kings, or even Luke or Romans – to say nothing of books such as Revelation, Job or Leviticus. Even knowing that the Holy Spirit is going to help us does not always mean that in practice we can see what the Bible is getting at. So much of it is quite different from life as we know it. Though we may not have the confidence to say it openly, some of us have niggling doubts as to whether a book so ancient really can say anything worthwhile in today's world. After all, any one of us can be in instant communication with people on the other side of the world through the wizardry of computer technology, while Jesus and Paul had never even seen something as basic as a bicycle. So why should we expect them to have any message for the world in the twenty-first century?

Some Christians – especially those of an older generation – will probably feel that such apparent problems are non-existent, or at least irrelevant. They can simply read the Bible, and instinctively know what God wants to say to them through it. If you fall into that category, you probably need read no further. But thank God for it – because your experience is certainly not typical of the majority even of your fellow believers, let alone those millions of others for whom, quite literally, the Bible is a closed book. Most of us have to battle with Bible reading. There are real problems for many people, and we need to face them honestly.

For some, the problem starts with the kind of book the Bible is. Preachers sometimes complain about people who take their theology from hymns and not from scripture. But when you think about it, the theology of most of our hymns is a lot more accessible than is the theology of the Bible. Just how *do* you extract a life-changing message out of books like Leviticus, or Ecclesiastes – or even Ezra or Jude? And what about the great challenges of our generation, most of which seem to be light years away from the concerns of the Bible writers – AIDS, environmental issues, genetic engineering, or even mundane things like career advice or guidance in personal relationships? These are the things on which Christians are searching for the will of God, and when young Christians read the Bible for the first time they are often perplexed and disappointed because it contains no ready-made answers to the kind of questions they are asking.

Just to intensify the perplexity, this apparent irrelevance of the Bible is not restricted to the more obscure parts of its contents. Even some central New Testament books seem at first sight to be afflicted by the same inadequacies. Take Galatians, for example. It contains a thorough and comprehensive answer to the question, 'Should I become a Jew and get circumcised in order to be a proper Christian?' If that's your question, then Galatians is just what you're looking for (though since circumcision is a male thing, even that excludes half the human race). But the bigger problem for most people is that they have not the slightest interest in wanting to know the answer to that sort of question. We have plenty of sexually-oriented questions, of course; questions like whether being a Christian entails also being heterosexual, or what kind of intimate relationships will be glorifying to God – but all that is in a different world altogether from the kind of questions Paul talks about in Galatians.

What then can we do about it? Some Christians give it up altogether as a worthless enterprise, and rely on their church or their friends to tell them whatever they might need to know in order to be good disciples of Jesus. Many more relegate the Bible to occasions when it seems necessary to act in some overtly 'religious' kind of way, but order their everyday lives in much the same way as others who are not committed to Christ. I have a good deal of sympathy with both those approaches, especially in the context of today's pressurized lifestyles. But how can we begin to move beyond such options? Let's start at the beginning with a very basic question. How should we read the Bible? I don't mean, how should we understand it, but how should we open the pages in order to get the feel of what is in them?

That may seem an odd question. You would need to be almost totally illiterate not to know that to read a book you start at the first page and go through to the end. Or would you? For in our Bible reading, Christians seem to have got into the strange habit of smashing the book up into so many little bits that a person who sits down to read an entire section of it through from start to finish is regarded as either eccentric or as some kind of super-saint. I'm not knocking the many excellent

9

Bible study aids that suggest you take a section of it at a time, and divide it up into daily bite-sized chunks. If it wasn't for them, maybe even fewer of us would attempt to read it! But if you always read a novel at the rate of a dozen lines a day, you wouldn't get very far, would you? You would certainly miss the buzz and excitement of what the author had written – especially if you started at page 120, then moved to page 25, followed by page 59! So why do we often read the Bible like this?

One perfectly good reason, of course, may be the fact that page 59 of the Bible happens to be separated from page 120 by a thousand years or more. For though the Bible presents a coherent picture of its subject – God and the relationship of spirituality to different aspects of human life and experience – it does so by setting out a variety of case studies, from different times, places and peoples, rather than containing a truly inter-connected story from start to finish. There is therefore a sense in which each section – or book – of the Bible is complete in itself. But that only serves to emphasise the importance of reading its various parts through in some kind of coherent way. If we skip from a story about Abraham, to one about David, and then jump over to the conversion of Paul, it will not be too surprising if we then find it hard to discern a continu-ous line of thought between them all. For the world of Paul was as different from Abraham's as today's digital world is from the Middle Ages. Consistent and consecutive reading of the Bible is always a helpful starting point.

It was the realisation of this simple fact that first opened my own eyes to some of the riches to be found in the Bible's pages. Indeed, my discovery that the Bible can be read in this way like any other book effectively marked the beginning of my own conscious commitment to the God of whom the Bible speaks – and had far-reaching repercussions for the whole course of the rest of my life.

As a teenager, I found myself a member of a family with a well-established pattern of church involvement. Everything seemed to revolve around the local church, in which my parents played an active part. As parents do, they took it for granted that I too would follow in their footsteps. From an early age, I was exposed to the Bible, and once I could read for myself it was assumed that I would make time for the daily exploration of its contents. I never found it a worthwhile or stimulating experience, and looking back I don't think most of the other people in the church did either. But they were all content to 'play the game', and so the challenges and difficulties were never mentioned, let alone explored. Even as a child, though, God had gifted me with a creative imagination, and I cannot remember a time when I did not ask what others might regard as 'awkward' questions about matters of faith. In relation to Bible reading, I was always struck by the way that predetermined Bible reading plans seemed to jump about from one bit of the Bible to another. Why, exactly, would three weeks on Abraham in Genesis be followed by a fortnight of the Sermon on the Mount, then six weeks on Romans – with a few days on the Prophets thrown in very occasionally for good measure? Everyone else I knew appeared to take it for granted that this was the appropriate way to make sense of this strange book, and that impression tended to be reinforced by most of the sermons I heard, delivered by earnest preachers who invariably seemed to have some special kind of knowledge of Scripture which enabled them to discern all manner of mysterious connections between what, to me, were apparently unrelated passages from books as diverse as Leviticus, Daniel and Hebrews. Though my peers seemed to regard all this as sophisticated and profound, I could never quite see the point of such connections myself, and by my early teens constant exposure to theological gymnastics of this kind had begun to turn me off the Bible altogether.

In the circumstances in which I found myself at the time, it would not have been a viable option for me to express my growing cynicism by refusing to go to church. A hard-headed pragmatism told me it would scarcely be worth all the hassle that would inevitably have followed such a course of action. Instead, my growing disillusionment with things religious in general, and with the Bible in particular, exhibited itself in deviant behaviour at school – especially in anything connected with Religious Education. By the time I was in year nine, I was the kind of obnoxious youth who regularly spent more time *outside* the classroom than in it. And I had an extensive repertoire of carefully conceived scenarios that were calculated to introduce maximum chaos into any class at minimum risk to myself.

You can imagine therefore that when a new and inexperienced teacher of religion arrived in my school, I was ready – no, eager – to exploit his vulnerability to the full. Even to this day I still recall my opening gambit when he first stepped through the classroom door. Rising to my feet as if making a maiden speech in Parliament, I said before my hushed peers (who were surreptitiously egging me on), 'Sir, I think you should know that this class has no time for religion, and no interest in the Bible.' To my surprise, he made straight for where I was sitting, placed his hands before me on the desk, and addressed me with that curious mixture of hesitation and recklessness that often seems to characterise unseasoned schoolteachers. 'Tell me, Drane,' he said, 'have you ever *read* the Bible?' I was left openmouthed. My bluff had been called, for the fact was that I had not in any serious way ever read the Bible at all. But, determined not to be out-manoeuvred, I went off that evening to try and read enough of it to be able to ask really awkward questions the next time.

I began with one of the Gospels – Mark. One thing that surprised me to begin with was the discovery that the whole Gospel could actually be read between the time when school finished for the afternoon and bedtime. Having made that discovery, I went back the next evening to read some more. This time it was Luke, as I recall, and then on subsequent evenings, Matthew and John. Then I moved on to Paul's letters, several of which can be read in as little as fifteen to twenty minutes. The discovery that it was actually possible to read the Bible in a way that made sense was exciting enough. But more significant was the sort of sense it began to make as soon as I did it the courtesy of taking it seriously. For in the process of reading the Gospels and other parts of the New Testament, I came face to face with a different Jesus than I had encountered before. This time, it was not a Jesus in a stained glass window, who was too good to be true. Nor was it a Jesus who was imprisoned and obscured in theological jargon, who was too complex to understand. Those two images were the Jesus I had already encountered in the church, and who meant nothing to me. But the Gospels presented a Jesus who seemed to be talking my language, addressing himself to the issues that concerned me, and (to my great surprise) speaking to me in a fresh and challenging way. 'John,' he was saying, 'I want your life. Just give me your life and see what I can do with it.'

I don't know that I fully understood what all that really meant at the time. But I knew this invitation made sense, and it was not long before religion was my favourite subject in school – and I had made the momentous decision to spend my student days in the study of theology, and the rest of my life in the service of Christ and his kingdom. I occasionally wonder where I would be today if I had never been confronted with that challenge. The fact that I made a personal discovery of Jesus Christ through reading the Bible has obviously had a far-reaching impact on my whole life. But apart from that I also learned a couple of simple facts about the Bible that are fundamental to any true understanding of its message.

First, I learned that the Bible is not all one book, but a series of books. To some of you that will be so obvious a thing that it is hardly worth mentioning. But it is a factor that has important repercussions for the way we read the Bible. For, despite what I have already said about jumping around in reading the Bible, it means that we will not necessarily make the best sense of it by reading all the books in their present order starting with Genesis and ending with Revelation. It also means that any one book needs to be looked at and thought about as a coherent whole within itself.

Then I also discovered how easy it is to read through an entire Bible book at one sitting. This is something many Christians find difficult to believe. But no matter how slowly you read, most people could get through even the longest of the Gospels (Luke) in a single evening – while several other New Testament books would take thirty minutes or less. Think of how many hours you will spend watching television or playing with the computer this week, and that will help to put your Bible reading in perspective. If you've never read whole Bible books like this before (and you'd be surprised how many haven't), try it and see for yourself. I am certain it will open up a new world of understanding – simply by reading it, let alone taking time to think about it. Inevitably, you may well wish to go over some parts in greater detail later on. You will certainly want to spend time just thinking of its implications and reflecting on its challenge to your own lifestyle. But that can most usefully come after you've given yourself a chance to see the broad sweep of any particular Bible book. Traditionally, Christians have done it the other way round: spending much time on the details, in the eventual hope of gaining a broad perspective. But I believe it is most effective to gain a wide bird's-eye view first, and then look more closely at the details in that context.

How then can we most helpfully read the Bible? I'll leave aside the question of translations, as that forms the subject of our next chapter. We all have our own favourites anyway. But it is going to be helpful to ask for what purpose you are reading the Bible on any given occasion. We can distinguish between at least two purposes in the life of most Christians. Many like to begin and/or end the day with a short statement from Scripture that can give something to reflect on as we go about our work. It may only be a single phrase – certainly not more than a few verses. This is reading the Bible for personal inspiration. We are looking for something that will remind us of some aspect of the gospel, and that will be easy to remember and think about. This sort of Bible reading is ideally served by daily Bible reading plans that direct you to a fairly short passage. If there is an element of continuity in such readings (for example, by going through the life and teaching of Jesus, or the life and letters of Paul), then so much the better. Unfortunately, not all Bible reading programmes do this, and sometimes they change direction with such frequency that they do not present much of a coherent picture at all.

Reading the Bible in order to study its message more consistently certainly requires continuity, so that whole books, or even whole collections of books, are studied and read in a consecutive manner. Here you will not find so much study material that is readily accessible. With one or two notable exceptions, you are less likely to find it organised on a daily basis. If you are looking for a more comprehensive understanding of Scripture, you will probably need to put in a bit more effort. But that is never wasted with the Bible. Nor is it something that is only for Christians who consider themselves bookish or even intellectual sorts of people. If we are serious in following Jesus, and if the Bible is truly important for our faith, then to read, think, and act upon it is going to be an essential part of our spiritual development. Though there will be many different ways both to read and hear the text, and to reflect on its message, a Christian who is by choice biblically illiterate is a contradiction in terms.

## Chapter 2

# Finding a useful map

One of the best ways I know to start an argument among Christians is to ask which is the best translation of the Bible. Just like our favourite washing powder or television programme, we generally think the version we habitually use is the best. In fact, we are less likely to change our Bible translation than our TV or our washing powder. For Christians of many years' standing, this is perhaps not the most crucial of issues. But for new Christians, faced with the challenge of regular Bible study, it is the most basic question of all: which Bible is the best one to use?

In this chapter, I want to share with you a part of the thrilling story of Bible translations down through the ages. It is an inspiring story of great courage and heroism. Men and women have suffered and died to have the Bible in their own language, and countless others have gone to extraordinary lengths of hardship to possess their own copy. Then we shall go on to ask what makes a good translation, before finally looking at some versions in wide use today, to try and discover which ones are the best, and why.

But before all that there is an even more basic question: why do we need a Bible to be *translated* at all? Professor C H Dodd, who was chairman of the panel which translated the *New English Bible* back in the 1960s, told in a TV interview of how he went to a typical English country parish, and decided to try out some of the first drafts of this version. After the Bible reading in the service, he told his congregation where it had come from, and invited their comments. One old lady approached him afterwards, saying, 'Well, it was very nice. But I don't know why you people are always wanting to change things. After all, if the King James Version was good enough for St. Paul, then surely it's good enough for us.'

In reality, the beginnings of Bible translation go back much further than the English Authorized (King James) Version of 1611. In fact, the need to translate the Bible can be traced right back to the days of the Old Testament itself. Towards the end of the Old Testament story, we find that the nation of Israel had come through a great crisis in their national life. Their territory had been invaded by the armies of the Babylonian emperor Nebuchadnezzar. The capital city of Jerusalem was devastated in 586 BC, and the leading citizens of the nation were taken away to live as exiles in Babylon itself. With its Temple and its royal dynasty gone, the heart was wrenched out of the nation. Yet hope was never lost. Those disorganized remnants of the population who were left behind in the homeland of Judah found life a constant struggle, though the exiles found life more comfortable, at least economically – and many of them set up businesses and other commercial enterprises in Babylon itself. Yet they were still painfully aware of the fact that they were rootless *émigrés*, who had been forcibly removed from the homeland they knew and loved, and were in great danger of losing their national identity and sense of self-respect. The depth of their feelings can be judged from Psalm 137, which must surely rank as one of the most heart-rending poems anywhere in literature.

It is a great tribute to their leaders that this exiled community not only survived, but also became the fertile ground out of which a renewed Jewish state was ultimately to arise. Determined not to forget their true origins, they set themselves to collect and study the traditional literature of their nation. History books, law books, messages from religious visionaries, poems and songs, were all carefully sifted through and reverently put together in fresh and creative ways in this period of national insecurity. Indeed, we largely owe the existence of the Old Testament in its present form to the enthusiasm and hard work of these far-sighted leaders of the exiled community in Babylon. They wanted to make sure that the great epic story of how God had dealt with their nation from the time of Abraham onwards, a thousand years earlier, would never be forgotten, and they preserved it as an inspirational narrative that would keep alive the possibility that one day they could again become a nation with their own land. Their opportunity for that came much sooner than they anticipated, for in less than fifty years after the occupation of Jerusalem by Nebuchadnezzar the Babylonian empire itself had collapsed, to be replaced by the more humane regime of the Persian emperor Cyrus. Babylonian policy had been to prevent con- quered nations ever regaining power by removing national leaders – and sometimes whole populations – from their home- lands, but the Persians saw things differently. Whereas the Babylonian regime was based on fear, Cyrus aimed to gain the support of others by more subtle means. To this end, he insti- tuted a repatriation programme, under which exiles who wished could return to the land of their birth, aided by gener- ous grants from the Persian government. Some of the Jews in Babylon jumped at the chance. The hiatus of the exile had, if anything, intensified their sense of nationhood, and they were eager to see their people returned to a measure of their former greatness. According to the Old Testament, they made the journey back to Palestine accompanied by a Persian official (Nehemiah) who would oversee the establishment of appropri- ate political systems, together with a Jewish priest called Ezra who would co-ordinate the moral and spiritual development of the people. One of the conclusions drawn during the time of exile was that Israel had suffered because of disobedience to God's will – and the leaders of this community were deter- mined that such a thing would never happen again.

The story of all this is to be found in the Old Testament books of Nehemiah and Ezra. It is a story of great economic and political challenges – and of cultural and religious sur- prises. The Old Testament scriptures which Ezra took back to Palestine with him had been written in Hebrew. This was the national language of the people, and had been the regular spo- ken tongue right up to the time of Nebuchadnezzar's invasion. So, naturally, this was the language in which the exiles in Babylon had edited and collated their books of history, poetry and celebration. But by the time Ezra returned with the Old Testament Law, the descendants of the Jewish population who had never left Jerusalem and Judah were no longer able to understand their national language, Hebrew. Instead, they spoke Aramaic, which was adopted as the official language of the Persian empire. Aramaic was not so very much different from Hebrew: it belonged to the same group of Semitic languages (along with Arabic and several other lesser known languages). But it immediately placed a barrier of understanding between the people and their traditional sacred writings.

Ezra's dream of a nation that would take God's Law seriously as the basis of its own life needed something else before it could come to fruition: it needed Bible translators, people who could take the Hebrew text of these books and make it accessible to those who now spoke only Aramaic. According to Nehemiah 8:7,8 this was an oral translation, given by interpreters who stood alongside Ezra as he read the Law in Hebrew. This tradition of spontaneous oral translation was to survive for several centuries, and by the time of Jesus it was commonplace for such Aramaic translations to be given as the Law was read (in Hebrew) in the synagogue week by week. Over the years, though, a more or less fixed (though by no means universally accepted) traditional Aramaic translation emerged, but it was not until well into the Christian era that any of this was written down, in a form that is now generally referred to as the Aramaic Targums ('translations') of the Old Testament. In their written form these all date from much later than the time of Jesus, but careful study of them has shed a good deal of light on the way both Jesus and the early Christians used and understood the Old Testament.

Even more important, however, was an early translation of the Old Testament into Greek. Though the main thread of the Old Testament story stops with those exiled Jews who returned to their homeland, many more (the majority) did not. Long before the time of Jesus, strong Jewish communities had taken root in all the major cities around the shores of the Mediterranean Sea. Naturally, they had to learn and use the language of the countries in which they settled, and following the conquests of Alexander the Great (333–323 BC), the whole Mediterranean world adopted Greek as the major language of international communication. It was only a matter of time before there were more Jews outside Palestine than within its borders. Even Palestine itself, as a part of Alexander's empire, soon adopted Greek ways of life, including the language. The use of Hebrew receded further and further into the background, and with it the need intensified for the Old Testament to be translated into a language that could readily be understood. The Jewish community which encouraged the translation of the scriptures into Greek was that of Alexandria in Egypt. According to one story, the project was actually sponsored by one of the Greek-speaking kings of Egypt, Ptolemy II Philadelphus (285-247 BC). Following the advice of the local Jewish leaders, he sent to Jerusalem for seventy men who knew both Hebrew and Greek, and locked them up in seventy individual cells while they got to work on the job of translation. When their work was finished, the king was amazed to discover that their seventy translations turned out to be identical, word-for-word – whereupon he instantly acknowledged that the books they were translating must indeed be the word of God! Not everyone believed that, even in the ancient world – and there are other stories which suggest that the translators worked in exactly the same way as we would today, in a committee. The truth is that no one really knows exactly when this Greek version was produced, and it may well be that it gradually emerged over an extended period of time as different parts of the Old Testament were translated piecemeal to meet the needs of the Jewish community. However it happened, the story of the seventy is permanently enshrined in the title by which we now refer to this Greek version of the Old Testament: the Septuagint ('work of the Seventy'), often abbreviated to LXX (the Roman number 70). This translation soon assumed a position of some importance. It was the Bible of the first Christians, most of whom were neither Jews nor could they read Hebrew. This version of the Old Testament was used by many of the writers of the New Testament itself – and it is an intriguing fact that, right from the very beginning, most Christians have always read the Old Testament only in translation!

The New Testament did not suffer from the same disadvantages, for it was initially written in Greek. Moreover, this was not the Greek of the classical historians and philosophers – which would have appealed only to a minority of people – but Greek as it was spoken and written in the everyday world of the marketplace, the army and the home. Many thousands of ordinary letters, both personal and commercial, have been discovered, which show that the New Testament was very much in the idiom of ordinary people. Faced with the challenge of communicating their message in a relevant way, the earliest Christians wrote and spoke in the way that ordinary non-Christian people did actually speak and write. That no doubt explains the enormous impact of their message, and it also has fascinating implications for the way we evaluate modern English translations of the Bible. If they are to be a true reflection of the original literary style of the New Testament, today's versions need to use the language of television and popular newspapers, rather than the measured tones of the classics of English literature!

In spite of the fact that the New Testament was written in the most widely spoken language of its time, the church grew so fast in those early centuries that fresh translations were soon required. Within a short time, the Bible had appeared in Latin, Syriac, Coptic, Gothic, Armenian, Ethiopic, Arabic, and other minor languages. Before long, the Bible appeared in English translation – Old English, to be precise, translated by the Venerable Bede (673–735), a monk from Jarrow in north-east England. It is uncertain just exactly how much he translated, for none of his work survives. But we do know that he began with the Gospel of John, and may well have completed the entire Bible by the time he died. However, the golden age of English Bible translation only began seriously with the work of John Wycliffe (1330–1384). Born in Yorkshire, he eventually became Master of Balliol College, Oxford, and in his day was one of the country's leading theologians. Up until that time, the church had always used the Bible in Latin, but Wycliffe saw that if the Word of God was to be of any use in shaping the lives of ordinary people, then it must speak in terms they could understand.

So he put in hand the translation of the Bible into English, which was subsequently used by wandering preachers who went from village to village through the English countryside.

Others were inspired by Wycliffe's example, in particular William Tyndale (1494–1536). Though he too was at home in Oxford and Cambridge, it was while working as a tutor in rural Gloucestershire that he became convinced of the need for an English Bible to be available in everyday language. He asked, 'Can one imagine a family where the children were unable to understand what their father says? If God spares my life, ere many years I will take care that a plough boy shall know more of the Scriptures than the bishop in his palace.' In collaboration with Miles Coverdale (1488–1569), Tyndale translated the entire New Testament into English, basing his work not only on the Latin but also on the various Greek texts that had recently become available in Europe. Tyndale did not live to see the whole Bible completed, but his friend Coverdale saw the work through, and the finished product was to have a formative influence on many subsequent English translations, even down to our own day. Those were hard times, and not everyone appreciated the endeavours of these early pioneers. Wycliffe was tried as a heretic, and spent the last months of his life in disgrace. Nor did the arguments end when he died: opposition to his English translation of the Bible was so strong that forty-four years after Wycliffe's death his body was dug up and the remains burned and thrown into a stream. Tyndale also suffered extreme deprivation for his part in Bible translation, being forced to leave England and find temporary refuge in Germany and Holland. Even there, he was not safe from those who opposed his work, and he was ultimately strangled and burned at the stake in the town of Vilvorde, not far from Brussels.

Of course, it was not solely because of their Bible translating that these men were so detested. There were many other political and ecclesiastical currents and cross-currents which led to their persecution, and their involvement in common-language Bibles came to be used as a yardstick to test other aspects of their loyalties. Nowadays, it would be unusual – though not unknown – for Bible translators to be personally vilified in this sort of way. But providing Bibles in the ordinary language of the street has aroused intense emotions in more recent times. When the Revised Standard Version first appeared in the USA in 1952, it was greeted by extraordinarily strong opposition even from within certain quarters of the Christian church. Professor Bruce Metzger was a widely-respected expert on the text of the New Testament, and was involved in its translation. One of the more curious objects he collected during his long career as a professor at Princeton Theological Seminary was a navy blue tin containing the ashes of the first RSV Bible to be incinerated in a public 'Bible burning ceremony'. Towards the end of 1952, the Rev M Luther Hux, minister of Temple Baptist Church at Rocky Mount, North Carolina announced that at the climax of his Sunday evening service he would set fire to a copy of the then-new RSV. At the time, Professor Thomas Frank – a friend of Professor Metzger, and himself also a theologian – was a student at the nearby Wake Forest College of North Carolina. He attended the service, and reported that the minister declared during the ceremony that the Bible, like the devil, was hard to burn – even with a blow torch! Not everyone shared such doubts about the new translation and by early December other local church leaders had issued a statement dissociating themselves from what they called 'the deplorable sacrilege of the burning of the Bible'. But that did not stop the opposition, and the anti-translation lobby soon gained momentum. On 29 January 1953, a protest rally attended by several thousands was held at the Met, at Broad and Poplar Street in Philadelphia. On that occasion the main speaker was Dr Kenneth Kinney, pastor of First Baptist Church, Johnson City, New York. He claimed that the RSV was part of 'Satan's threefold master plan', which included capturing the political, economic and religious leadership of the world; taking over the churches through religious institutions (such as councils of churches); and influencing the opinions of ordinary Christians through new Bible translations. Phases one and two, he claimed, had already been accomplished – and with the advent of the RSV, the final stage of the devil's jigsaw had fallen into place. He claimed as proof of this the fact that (in his view) the translators were all Communists or Communist sympathisers. When challenged to substantiate this charge, he pointed to Hebrews 1:9. In the older King James version, this reads: 'God... hath anointed thee with the oil of gladness above thy fellows'. The RSV was almost identical, except that 'fellows' there became 'comrades' – and who, asked Dr Kinney, would use such a word, other than Marxist revolutionaries?

The RSV is not the only modern version to have stirred up such remarkable passions. When the New Testament part of the Good News Bible was first published in 1966, many people found it was just what they wanted. For the first time, the Bible was in a language that was simple and dignified, yet accessible even to the youngest reader. Many Christians bought copies for mass distribution, among them the churches of Cabarrus County, North Carolina. In spring 1970 they distributed 40,000 free copies of the New Testament. But what was Good News for some was not so good for others, and in no time at all another group of twenty churches had got together to demonstrate their disapproval with yet another public burning ceremony. This time the opposition was led by Rev H Lloyd Walters, of Gordon Heights Baptist Church, Concord, North Carolina. When the appointed hour for the burning came, on Sunday 28 June 1970, he decided instead to turn it into a mock funeral. Copies of the Good News Bible (New Testament) were ceremonially carried out of his church and buried. He too denounced those who wanted to make the Bible available in everyday language, referring in his sermon to their work as 'the masterpiece of the devil'. Whether the Bible should speak in the language of ordinary people continues to stir up intense feelings, especially in certain parts of the USA. It is probably true to say that in Britain modern translations have been more widely accepted, though even here there is a strong rearguard action being fought by some who would like to preserve the ethos of the Book of Common Prayer and the Bible that it influenced, the King James, or Authorised Version.

On the whole, however, people can see the sense in the Bible being made available in ordinary language. Even in the turbulent political atmosphere of sixteenth-century Britain, it was not long after Tyndale's time before it was taken for granted that, if the Bible was to have any relevance, it must speak in words people could understand. At a meeting of the Sixth Scots Parliament, convened in Edinburgh on 20 October 1579 by King James VI, an act was passed requiring every householder above a certain income to make available a Bible 'in vulgar language... for the better instruction of themselves and their families, in the knowledge of God'. The penalty for not doing so was a £10 fine – and government inspectors were appointed to make sure that the decree was observed! This was the same King James who was to play a major role in the development of Bible translations, for James VI of Scotland was also James I of England, and it was under his patronage that the renowned Authorised (King James) Version of the Bible was translated and published in 1611. Though based on what would now be regarded as inferior Greek manuscripts, that version set the standard for all subsequent English translations of the Bible – and was to be the means whereby the Bible was recognized as one of the great classics of all time.

What, then, makes a good translation of the Bible? Four things are vital. First, authenticity. It is important that the ancient texts from which the translators work should themselves be as accurate as possible. The Hebrew and Greek originals were written long before the invention of printing, and every ancient manuscript had to be laboriously copied out by hand. This inevitably introduced the possibility of simple scribal error – and since none of the original Bible manuscripts, written by the authors themselves, now survive, we need to be sure that the copies we work from are as accurate as possible. This is not as difficult as it seems. Some Bible manuscripts are very old indeed, and go back to within a generation or two of when the books were written. But our evidence for the Bible is far more extensive than what we know of any other document of comparable age. For example, all the classical Greek and Latin authors are known only through manuscripts dating from many hundreds of years after they lived. But there are literally thousands of manuscripts of the Bible that are both early and reliable, and we have no reason at all to doubt that the Greek and Hebrew texts commonly used today are in every respect completely authentic.

But then, a good translation must also be accurate. It is important that the Hebrew and Greek should be translated as carefully as possible. One of the more painful memories of my schooldays is of hours spent painstakingly working through dictionaries trying to find English words that would be an accurate rendering of French, German and Latin. What I ended up with was always a translation – of a sort. Quite often it was not an intelligible one, because good translation needs far more than the replacing of one foreign word by one English word. In the case of the Bible, making an accurate translation involves gaining a thorough understanding of the way Hebrew and Greek words were actually used in different contexts. It requires careful thought about the way we use our own language, and an imaginative combining of the two.

Intelligibility is the third hallmark of a good translation. The translator always stands astride two worlds, and two cultures. Sometimes there are more than two – for the culture of the New Testament, though basically Greek and Roman, contained strong undercurrents of Old Testament thinking and the culture in which that had its origins. This can create particular difficulties at the points where our culture has little that corresponds with some particular feature of the Bible world. Sacrifice is a good example of this. Not only was it part and parcel of the whole fabric of life, but it also had its own highly specialised vocabulary. In Hebrew and Greek, the difference between 'propitiation' and 'expiation' would have meant something, for both were technical terms used to express what was thought to be happening in certain sorts of sacrifices. But in modern English, neither term means anything at all – nor, for that matter, does the very notion of sacrifice convey anything very helpful to most people. The translator must face problems like this, and resolve them in such a way that accuracy is preserved, while still producing a translation that can readily be understood. This is an enormous challenge, but it is the key to good translation. If you need to consult an English dictionary to find out what the translation means, then it is a bad translation!

Reliability is the fourth characteristic of a good translation. Can the translators be trusted to have done their job properly? Have they gone about their work responsibly? Or have they allowed translation to become obscured and merged with interpretation, thereby imposing their own religious beliefs on the Bible? Unfortunately, this sometimes happens. The Jehovah's Witnesses, for example, found it exceedingly difficult to justify their beliefs on the basis of commonly accepted translations of the Scriptures – and so they made their own, the New World Translation. Not surprisingly, it is a good deal easier to 'prove' their distinctive theology from this than it would be from, for example, the RSV. Another striking example of a translation where the translator's own preferences got the better of the text was in James Moffatt's New Translation of the Bible, which appeared complete in 1928. Moffatt was a theological professor, much attracted by theories that suggested the text of the Bible had been subjected to corruptions and dislocations. These he tried to 'correct' in his translation – with the result that it is often difficult to relate his version to other, more conventional translations. Moffatt himself told the story of how he arrived to deliver a lecture one night in a small town in the USA, and the poster outside the hall proclaimed: 'Author of Bible to lecture here tonight'. There was at least a grain of truth in that scribal mistake!

Even more recent translations seem to proceed on similar assumptions. The translators of the New King James Version, for example, in their preface actually make a virtue out of the fact that they based their work on unreliable and outdated manuscripts (the so-called Received Text), and then go on to explain how, unlike certain other (unidentified) modern versions, theirs is designed to back up particular theological interpretations of the Bible's meaning. But even more mainstream translators have occasionally done the same thing: for example, the reference to Andronicus and Junia in Romans 16:7 was regularly translated as 'men of note among the apostles', even though Junia could be nothing but a woman's name – but this suited scholars who could not conceive of any woman having that kind of status in the early church. There is nothing wrong with asking about the Bible's meaning – that is what this book is about. But to build a particular view of it into a translation is a very dangerous procedure. If we are not careful, we soon become more concerned with making the Bible back up what *we* think, than with exposing our ideas to the challenge and change which scripture as God's word should bring.

Finally, we must take a brief look at some of the translations most frequently used today. Which is the best Bible to use? Like other apparently simple questions, this can be a slippery one to handle. We need to ask ourselves: best for what purpose? Obviously, any useful Bible translation will need to express the ideas of the original texts in such a way that their meaning and impact for people today will be roughly the same as it was for the original readers. There have been several schools of thought regarding the most effective way to accomplish this. Some, motivated by a profound reverence for the actual words of Scripture, have insisted that the only authentic way to be faithful to the Bible writers and their original intentions is to translate their books word-for-word. Others point out that this can create a very stiff translation, not only because many Hebrew and (especially) Greek terms have no exact equivalent in contemporary English (and therefore a single word might need a phrase or even a complete sentence to explain it), but also because sentence structures in English are quite different from these ancient languages, and therefore to replicate the style of the original text exactly can easily produce a rendering that, far from enlightening today's readers, might actually result in misunderstandings, if not total mystification. This is why almost all the most recent translations have chosen to translate ideas, rather than just words, in the hope of producing a text that will be easy to read and understand as well as accurately communicating the meaning of the original Hebrew and Greek.

# The Authorised Version

For three centuries, this was the only English Bible in widespread use at all. Translated at the request of King James in 1611, it was the literary successor to the work of William Tyndale. But it established new standards of careful scholarship, and has carved out for itself a unique place in the history of English literature. Along with the plays of William Shakespeare, it has become an immortal symbol of one of the great classical ages of the English language. No doubt this would have surprised the forty-seven men who produced it, for in their preface they acknowledge that while they had utilised the most accurate texts then known, their work would only be temporary, as fresh discoveries gave new insight into the biblical languages. Their caution in this respect was largely unheeded, and though their work had its critics it gained an affection in the hearts of English readers which still survives to this day.

There can be no denying that to hear certain passages read from this version in the context of some great ceremonial occasion can be a moving experience. But nowadays its appeal must be confined to the aesthetic power of its English style, for as a useful translation of the Bible its value is strictly limited. It scores badly on almost all the tests of a good translation. This is partly because of our increased knowledge about the Bible and its world. Much new information about the New Testament in particular has come to light since 1611, and all the most ancient documents have been discovered in the last 150 years or so. In addition, we now have a much greater understanding of the meanings of both of the biblical languages, especially Hebrew. English usage has also changed a lot, and is evolving all the time as it becomes a more global language. The Authorised Version was written in the language of its own day, and reflects English usage in the age of Elizabeth I. Many of its words are no longer a part of the English language, and today's readers would need a glossary to explain their true meaning. This immediately constructs a very real barrier for the majority of those who come to the Bible hoping that God will address them through its pages in words they can understand.

# New Revised Standard Version

This is a more up-to-date translation, with its origins in the Revised Standard Version published in the USA in 1952. The 'Standard' which was revised then was the American Standard Version of 1901, which in turn was very similar in language and concept to the English Revised Version of 1885 – and which in turn took the Authorised Version as its basic starting point. So the NRSV stands very much in the Tyndale – AV line, while taking account of newer textual and linguistic insights.

At the time of its first appearance in the 1950s, the RSV was a new translation, though the translators consciously set out to preserve the lofty language of their eminent predecessors. For example, they retained the ancient forms 'thee' and 'thou' in references to God, which gave it the same feel as the AV, though of course it did not suffer from the same unintelligibility – and things like paragraph divisions were introduced for the first time in the RSV. The further revision of this version in 1989 which produced the New Revised Standard Version was, in effect, a fresh translation altogether from the original Hebrew and Greek texts. While it aimed to be a literal translation, the translators set out to get rid of archaic words (including references to God), and to take account of the ways in which English terminology had changed over the years. They also sought to make it the first translation to adopt consistently gender-inclusive language, which meant that instead of using traditional male-oriented terminology that might refer to Christians as 'brothers' or to people in general as 'mankind', they substituted words that included both men and women. But they stopped short of using such inclusive terminology of God, still perpetuating the use of male pronouns in that connection, even though the translators acknowledged that the God of whom the Bible speaks is, technically, without gender, and therefore neither male nor female.

This careful updating of linguistic usage, without abandoning traditional conventions, has been regarded as a particular commendation of this version for public reading in a church context. Its ponderous language is clear, and yet has the weight of added dignity that is often thought to be important for Christian worship. The NRSV has also established itself as a useful Bible for serious study, because it follows the Hebrew and Greek texts very closely, and so it is possible to identify particular points of interpretation quite readily.

## New International Version

Completed in 1978, with subsequent minor revisions, this version has found most favour among conservative Protestants – at whose instigation it was originally commissioned. According to its preface, the impetus for its production arose largely out of a dissatisfaction with other modern translations. The aim was to produce a version that would be accurate, and reflect current English usage, while attempting to preserve a literary quality that would make it suitable for public reading in churches, as well as private study. Its popularity suggests that for many people it has met these aims – though its English style is hardly cast in the popular idiom of everyday English, either in Britain or the USA.

But what is more distinctive about this version is the stated aim of its translators to produce a translation that would enhance a conservative view of the Christian message. In their preface they write of their own commitment to 'the authority and infallibility of the Bible as God's word in written form'. In this sense their procedure was significantly different from that of the NRSV team, who did not begin with a particular theological stance, but simply with a desire to translate the Hebrew and Greek of the Bible into relevant modern English.

## The New English Bible/Revised English Bible

Unlike the NIV, which was the brainchild of a small group of like-minded individuals, the New English Bible was very much the product of the mainstream churches in Britain. As long ago as 1946 the Church of Scotland saw the need for a new translation into 'standard' English, something that would stand the test of time and could take its place alongside the Authorised Version as one of the classics of English literature. The support of other British churches was enlisted, and the finished work eventually appeared in 1970. It was produced by a team of very fine scholars, under the general direction of Professor C H Dodd. In parts, the NEB was indeed a fine, clear translation in good contemporary English – especially some parts of the New Testament. But much of the Old Testament was dull, and in its original form its partiality for scholarly fashions in Old Testament study – some of which soon passed – mitigated against its permanence. Though most of these quirks were eliminated when it was revised in 1989 and relaunched as the Revised English Bible, it has never quite captured the spirit and vitality of the original texts, and has not managed to establish itself as a version with strong popular support.

## The Jerusalem Bible

This version has an unusual history, which began at the Dominican Biblical School in Jerusalem, with the preparation of an annotated French translation of the Bible. This was completed in the mid-1950s, and was so popular that it inspired the idea of an English version along the same lines. Naturally, the English was not translated from the French, but with due reference to the original languages. As a translation, it is clear, readable, and reliable. It makes no claim to literary excellence, aiming rather for a simple directness of expression, based closely on the actual words of the Hebrew and Greek texts. As such, it is a useful translation for serious Bible study.

But its major distinctiveness is to be found in the comprehensive introductory and textual notes which it contains. Each Bible book is preceded by an explanation of its background and contents, while the text itself is helpfully illustrated by extended marginal notes throughout. These study aids were all translated from the original French edition, and they help to give the Jerusalem Bible a unique place among English versions. Naturally, the notes in any study Bible tend to reflect the approach of the editors and the Jerusalem Bible is no exception. The notes, however, fairly represent the mainstream of contemporary biblical scholarship, and probably no other comparable volume has so much useful information. To buy one is to acquire a whole theological library in miniature.

Like other translations, it continues to be updated and revised. The New Jerusalem Bible appeared in English in 1985, and a third French edition is currently in preparation, which will no doubt appear in English in due course.

## Good News Bible

The Good News Bible is quite different in concept from any of the others mentioned so far, since it is based on the principle of 'dynamic equivalence translation'. Most other translations essentially follow the constructions of the original Hebrew and Greek texts. A dynamic equivalence version tries to take the impact that the text would have originally made, and transfer that accurately into an appropriate English idiom so as to make the same impression on the modern reader.

This is not the same as a paraphrase, in which extra words of explanation may well be inserted into the text. Nor is it a particularly new idea, and in relation to the history of Bible translating it goes back to the Reformer, Martin Luther, who wrote: 'Whoever would speak German must not use Hebrew style. Rather he must see to it – once he understands the Hebrew author – that he concentrates on the sense of the text, asking himself, Pray, tell, what do the Germans say in such a situation? Once he has the German words to serve the purpose, let him drop the Hebrew words and express the meaning freely in the best German he knows.' Luther's German Bible was a great success, and the GNB has also been. If sales figures are anything to go by, it is the most successful of all modern translations, and has undeniably played a major part in communicating the Bible's essential message to new generations of readers.

Inevitably, it has its detractors. An eminent Scottish divinity professor is reported to have commented on first seeing it: 'It's not good; it's not news; and it's not a Bible!' But such cynicism is not shared by others, who have found that its clear English, remarkably free from theological and ecclesiastical jargon, has for the first time in their lives brought them face to face with God in a fresh way. For reading whole books of the Bible through, the GNB can hardly be bettered. But it is by no means deficient for more detailed Bible study either.

## New Century Version

This was originally published in an illustrated form as *The International Children's Bible* (1986), but its appeal to a broad cross-section of readers of all ages soon led to its appearance as a separate Bible version. Like other modern versions, it was translated by a panel of experts from the original Hebrew and Greek texts, and aimed from the outset to be a 'dynamic equivalence' translation (like the GNB), rather than providing a more literal rendering. For its first edition, the style of English used had been carefully scrutinised to ensure that its vocabulary would readily be understood by primary school students, and that has continued, with ancient customs also being explained either in the text, or in footnotes. Like the NRSV, the NCV avoids the use of male language in those places where the text refers to people more generally, though (again like the NRSV) it retains male pronouns in references to God. As well as being a reliable translation, the NCV is also a very readable version, and lends itself particularly well to consecutive reading of extended sections of the Bible books.

## Contemporary English Version

This version, published in 1995, is another dynamic equivalence translation. Its main distinctive feature is that its translators began from the observation that language is always spoken before it is written down, and that many people today are more likely to hear the Bible being read by someone else than they are to read it for themselves. Special attention has therefore been given to the expressions used to ensure that – while remaining faithful to the original Hebrew and Greek texts – this version will be easy to read and to listen to, conveying the message of the Bible's authors in contemporary English that is not only accurate, but also lucid and lyrical. The appearance of the text on the printed page has also been designed for easy access, and this is one of the very few translations to be printed in the same way as a normal book, instead of having each page divided into two columns of text alongside each other. This makes for easy reading of narratives, and also gives more flexibility in relation to the way in which poetic passages can be set out, with the length of individual lines being determined only by the structure and sense of the poetry, rather than being dependent on the cramped space afforded by narrow columns of type. In this way the translators have endeavoured to replicate not only the meaning of the texts, but also the impact they may have had on their first readers.

## The New Living Translation

Launched in 1996, this is the work of more than ninety scholars, mostly from North America but with a few British people also involved. Like most other recent translations, it adopts the method of translating 'dynamic equivalence', rather than rendering each Hebrew or Greek word. It has been widely welcomed as an easy-to-read version, especially for young people, and has been published in many different guises aimed at different markets. It is, in effect, the work of a committee, though one of its more unusual features is that the individual translators are each identified with the books on which they worked. Unlike some others, which preserve references to things like ancient weights and measures, or ways of telling the time, this one replaces all such indications with modern (American) forms of expression. Apart from the book of Psalms, it also sets out Hebrew poetry as if it were straightforward narrative, a feature which some consider to be going beyond the bounds of what should be appropriate in accurate translation. What was exclusively male language in the original texts has been adapted to conform to present-day usage of gender-inclusive language, though references to God preserve male pronouns. Whereas in some other translations, this convention has been followed only because scholars believe English usage is not yet generally ready for a change in this respect, the translators of the NLT state that, for them, 'essential traits of God's revealed character can only be conveyed through the masculine language expressed in the original texts of Scripture'.

Like other dynamic equivalence translations, this one is inevitably of limited usefulness to readers who want to have direct access for themselves to the types of words and technical religious terminology that was regularly used in the original Greek and Hebrew texts. But only a minority of people are typically looking for that, and most will be satisfied with a version that, in general, provides a reasonably accurate account in modern language of what the Bible's authors were trying to say. The NLT certainly meets that need.

Which one is the best to use? That is always going to be an emotive question, with many variables, and any answer must reflect personal expectations and preferences. But for a general all-round Bible, the Good News must come near the top of the list. Its simplicity of expression has never quite been improved on by other translations, and it manages to give something of the feel of the ancient texts without becoming ponderous and impenetrable. On those occasions when more specific knowledge of particular Biblical expressions is important, it can if necessary be supplemented by something like the NRSV, NCV or Jerusalem Bible, all of which preserve a more literal connection with the actual words used by the original authors.

## Chapter 3

# The shape of the land

Reading the Bible is important, and doing so in a translation that uses language that is simple to understand is vital. But it's one thing to read it – quite another to understand what it is all about. Even when the words themselves make sense, penetrating their relevance and meaning is often easier said than done. For many people, Bible reading is like trying to squeeze milk out of a coconut: you know there's something in there, but getting it out can be a bit of a problem if you don't happen to possess the right tools, and know how to use them. Presumably that explains why even Christians often give up altogether – or, if we do not quite give up, we rather tend to restrict our reading to comfortable and familiar passages. As a result, many regular Bible readers still have only a very narrow knowledge of what is actually in the Bible, let alone what we might then do with it.

Of course, it is possible to go to the opposite extreme and merely specialise in knowledge of the details. I remember when I was a teenager, one of the more mindless activities of church youth groups was the sort of Bible quiz which specialised in detailed knowledge of the irrelevant and the unimportant. Mind you, it could be exciting enough – especially if you happened to be the one who actually knew the identity of Jochabed's mother-in-law, or who it was that impaled a visitor to the ground with a tent peg through his head! But this kind of obsession with the curious and the unusual soon reduces the Bible to a form of Trivial Pursuit, and can actually inoculate you against ever expecting that God could speak through it in a way that might have any direct application for everyday living. It might seem so obvious as hardly to be worth saying, but if you never read the Bible in a serious way, then you are not very likely to make much of it. Yet, sadly, many people can claim to know exactly 'what the Bible says' on any number of subjects, without actually giving much attention to reading it for themselves. It never ceases to amaze me how many even of those who are in training for the Christian ministry seem to imagine that they can get to grips with its message without actually reading it! They will read books about the Bible in their dozens – Bible histories, atlases, commentaries, concordances, dictionaries – but will they read the Bible itself? Not if they can possibly avoid it!

It is a dangerous idea to suppose that we can know what God requires without taking some account of the teaching of the Scriptures, especially when 'what the Bible teaches' then becomes enshrined in the habits and practices of Christian groups where no-one ever bothers to go back to the text to see if that is truly the case. This attitude was one of the major shortcomings of the Pharisees. They organised their beliefs and practices largely on the basis of rules handed down from previous generations, rules that were supposed to be a summary of what the Old Testament taught. It was precisely their unthinking acceptance of what they had been told that led to Jesus' criticisms of them. Many of these rules, he observed, were not actually representative of God's will at all, but were simply 'the traditions of the ancestors' (Mark 7:8–13). It is all too easy to make the same sort of mistakes today, and most of us do from time to time. We imagine that because certain notions are traditional parts of Christian belief or custom, handed on in the church, that automatically means that they must be based in the Bible. But 'what the church says' – especially 'what *my* church says' – is not always the same thing as 'what the Bible says'. For centuries, Christians affirmed that slavery was part of God's will. Those who bought and sold African slaves in the southern states of the USA were for the most part committed Christians. They were certainly supported by official Christian stances, for though there was spasmodic debate about the subject – especially among Quakers and Methodists – the vast majority of (white) Christians on both sides of the Atlantic had no hesitation in asserting that slavery was a perfectly natural institution, and was part of the way God intended the world to operate. The 'evidence' for that was found in the Bible, especially in the stories of the early chapters of Genesis. Nowadays, most

Christians would think they were mistaken – though there are still pockets of the American churches where people believe that racial segregation is in accordance with the will of God. But these people were making a very simple mistake. They confused the teaching of their church, and what was culturally congenial for them, with the teaching of the Bible. It is an easy thing to do.

So how do we get through to what God is actually saying in the Bible? This is a deceptively simple question, and is much easier to ask than it is to answer. One of the most vivid memories of my childhood is of being taken to a Bible discussion meeting at which the main topic of debate was (if you can believe it) whether it was right for Christians to own dogs! You might think that such a question would hardly raise any great theological or spiritual principles. Still less might you expect to find any guidance on the matter in the Bible. You might even question whether Christians need to spend their time in deep and serious disputation about such matters. But I remember one prominent speaker on that occasion who not only considered it a topic worthy of solemn investigation, but was quite sure that the possession of a dog represented a grave dilution of one's Christian testimony. The reason he gave was that, according to Revelation 22:15 (AV), 'without are dogs, and sorcerers, and whoremongers, and murderers...', together with other assorted undesirables. Not content with this one text, he then went on to refer to a whole variety of passages in which dogs appear doing various unsavoury things. To cap it all, he made much play on an odd statement in 2 Peter, to the effect that 'The dog is turned to his own vomit again.' I can only imagine what other things he expounded after that, for at that point I burst into uncontrollable laughter and had to be removed from the sombre gathering. But the whole episode clearly made a lasting impression on my youthful mind, for whenever I was subsequently taken to listen to that particular preacher (who was apparently reckoned to be an able speaker), I could think of nothing but the habits of undisciplined dogs!

You may be tempted to think that, with so much evident confusion even among those who seem to have given some thought to the matter, there is little hope for the ordinary punter. It is certainly true that, for those who are sufficiently determined, it is apparently possible to 'prove' just about anything by selecting the appropriate Bible text. But to proceed in this way is actually to do violence to the very book which we are supposed to be acknowledging as our authority. There is an old saying, 'A text without a context is a pretext'. Many a Bible study or church sermon could be rescued from triviality if more of us remembered that. Much personal Bible reading could also be revitalised if we discovered what that means in practical terms. We can begin to appreciate this by thinking for a moment about the very nature of the Bible itself. In the world of religious writings, it is certainly distinctive. For one thing, it is in reality not one book, but a collection of books – sixty-six of them in all. Moreover, few of their authors knew any of the other authors, while none of them ever expected their work to be collected in an anthology that would form the scriptural basis of the Christian faith. This is one thing that sets the Bible apart from the scriptures of other world faiths, which tend to be more or less systematic and philosophical presentations of religious and moral ideas. There are books of a similar type in the Christian tradition – but the Bible is not one of them. If you want this kind of analytical exploration of what Christianity is all about, then you need to look for the confessions, creeds, and books of systematic theology that have been the theologians' stock-in-trade from the very earliest centuries of the church's history. All these take their starting point from the Bible, but in important respects are quite different from it.

The Bible is a multi-dimensional book. It does of course contain insights into the nature of God, and how people might get to know God, but these are never presented in the form of theological statements as such. The Bible's teaching is embodied in several quite diverse literary forms. At first sight, much of the Bible looks like history. But a closer inspection shows that history is only a part of it. If a modern librarian was trying to classify the Bible's books for the first time, it is most unlikely that they would all end up on the same shelves. History, biography, law, songs, poetry, and letters are all easy to recognise, but there are other items whose character is less obvious. For example, the books of the prophets: are they sermons, or political pamphlets, or what? Or books like Jonah, Esther and Ruth: are they fiction or non-fiction, drama or narrative, poetry or prose? There are others such as Daniel and Revelation which raise different kinds of questions for the modern reader who tries to classify them according to their literary style, or genre.

Inevitably, all this means that if we are to understand the essential message of the Bible, we need to discover something about the background of its various parts. It is neglect of this simple fact that can allow otherwise intelligent Christians to spend half a day debating what the Bible has to say about the relations between dog ownership and spirituality! But it can also lead to more fundamental and far-reaching errors than that. In the course of history, by far the majority of Christian-based cults and deviant belief systems have arisen from the same sort of misunderstandings. Take the Jehovah's Witnesses as an example. A key element in their practices is the refusal to allow any of their members – or their children – to receive blood transfusions. According to them, this is forbidden in various Bible passages, such as Leviticus 7:26,27; 17:10–14; and Acts 15:29. In reality, of course, it would have been impossible for the Bible to make any mention at all of blood transfusions, for the technology required to make them possible was unknown in the ancient world. But more than that, even a nodding acquaintance with the actual cultural context of the various passages that are supposed to relate to this issue soon reveals that they deal with a totally different situation, involving ancient beliefs about sacrifice and other rituals that again play little part in the life of the modern world. Of course, there are still some societies today which are not so different from the thinking of the ancient Hebrews at this point. But for most people – certainly those living under the influence of western thinking and culture – it is not easy to take up such passages and see their immediate relevance to contemporary concerns. Some would question whether they have any relevance at all, but everyone would be agreed that their interpretation is a complex matter, requiring us to take careful account of their original meaning before we can begin to apply them to the totally different circumstances of our own day.

Our understanding of even apparently straightforward things can be radically affected by the way we understand their context in the Bible. When Abraham and his wife Sarah concluded that they could have no children, they without hesitation secured another sexual partner for Abraham, by whom a child was subsequently born (Genesis 16). Elsewhere, in both Old and New Testaments, Abraham is acclaimed as a great hero of faith. Does this then mean that Christians should deal with childlessness in the same way? Is Abraham's behaviour a primitive example of the modern debate about surrogacy? And if not, how should we understand it? Like many other aspects of the Bible, the answer to all those questions is to be found in an adequate understanding of the historical and cultural context in which the story itself is set. We will look at the context of this particular story shortly, for without that it is easy to jump to conclusions that are not related to the true concerns of the text.

The idea that the Bible needs to be set against its proper context in order to be understood fully is nothing new, but some Christians think it is all a matter only for experts. This however is a head-in-the-sand attitude, and gives undue deference to the so-called 'experts'. In any case, a moment's thought will show that with anything we read one of the first questions we ask is: what would these words mean in the context in which they are written? So why not ask the same question with the Bible? The context, or 'life setting' of any piece of writing or speech is always an essential part of its meaning. Take away the context, and quite often you can't be certain exactly what the words mean. Think, for example, of the word 'saved'. If you hear that in church on Sunday morning, the person using it will likely be referring to some spiritual experience. Even then, that particular terminology would not be universally acceptable in all churches: others might speak instead of 'conversion', or 'commitment', or simply 'being a Christian'. In spite of such variations, though, if you then go to a soccer match on Sunday afternoon and hear somebody shouting about 'being saved', you can be pretty sure that this is not a reference to religion. Rugby fans, sitting at home savouring the replays of an exciting international game on the television, might well have their own equivalent of that, when the commentator describes a certain move as 'a great conversion'. Once again, he is unlikely to be talking about some sort of Damascus road experience that has taken place on the pitch.

That is all commonplace, and none of us really need a book on the Bible to draw our attention to it, for in everyday life we automatically tell the difference between the various uses of these words, without giving a second thought to what is going on. The fact is that we are so familiar with the different contexts in which we use words today that it is no effort at all to distinguish them and come up with a true interpretation of what is going on in any given circumstance. But when it comes to the Bible, we do not have the same easy familiarity with its world, or its language – or for that matter its writers and their first readers. Before we can react to its message in the same instinctive way that we respond to what happens around us every day, we need to make some conscious effort to learn about the Bible's world for ourselves. This will be a first step towards gaining some idea of how and why these ancient people responded to the presence of God in their lives – and that in turn should assist us in grasping what God might be saying to us now through their experiences.

Another topic, this time related to church organisation, highlights the same need. When churches today appoint people they call 'deacons', what should their role be in the life of the church? It would be easy enough to look up a few scattered passages in the New Testament where the term is used, and to go on from there to work out some sort of answer to our question. That has usually been the standard way for Christians to proceed, and so it is not difficult to identify apparently 'scriptural' arguments to support both the practice of the Anglican community, where a 'deacon' is a member of the ordained ministry, and the rather different position of the English free churches, where 'deacons' would typically be lay people! In point of fact, if we were to look closely at the New Testament's use of this terminology in its own social and theological context, we would almost certainly discover it has little in common with either of these widely-held perceptions. Christians get themselves into the same sort of muddle on other matters, such as the nature of relationships between women and men in the church. On the face of it, if (as the New Testament seems to say) freedom and equality are of the essence of the gospel, then one might suppose that these qualities ought to characterise relationships between the sexes in the work of the church. But we all know that other issues inevitably surface when Christians discuss in detail the role of women in the church (why do they never argue about the role of men, I wonder?). Here again, it is easy enough to gather together a few Bible passages which seem to relate to the topic, but understanding them is not the same thing as merely collating them. The same thing is true of debates about sexual orientation and related matters. If we truly want to hear what God would say to us on the subject, we need to consider the whole context – not just the literary and theological context, but the social context in which the New Testament was written.

Now that we have some of the problems in sharper focus, we need to begin looking in detail at this business of the Bible's context. Christians often imagine that getting to the bottom of life in Bible times is no more difficult than it would be for a British family to settle in, say, the USA. Yes, there are differences – differences of money, politics, education, and language. The differences can be unsettling at first, especially if you don't know what to ask for. British visitors to the US need to remember to pump 'gas' into their cars rather than 'petrol', and to think of their streets as the 'neighborhood'. Sometimes it can get embarrassing: any British visitor who attempts to buy an old-fashioned English 'rubber' will soon discover that it is really an 'eraser' they want ('rubbers' being something quite different). If employees request a 'hike', then instead of reaching for heavy boots to go on a long walk (as they would in Britain), their employers (they hope) will give them a pay increase. In the end, though, it's not too difficult to make sense of all this. In any event, all British people think they already know what America is like, even if they've never been there. Haven't we seen it all on the small screen in our own living rooms? The same thing is true not only of the US, but of other world cultures with much less in common with our own.

Life in the world of the Bible, however, was nothing like this. Instant communication in those days and places was totally unheard of. It is easy to read of Paul travelling around most of southern Europe, and imagine him doing it in the same way as today's tourists. Apart from the fact that he was very much an exception among the early Christians, travel was not too easy for him in any case. It was certainly more straightforward than it had once been, for the Romans built magnificent roads and established regular sea routes to link the various bits of their empire. But technology in today's sense was a thing of the future. Even something as simple as the bicycle would have been a mind-bending invention for the people of Bible times – and an ordinary person must have had very limited knowledge of the world beyond their own community.

Simple facts like this could have far-reaching social and political consequences. In the time of Jesus, if the emperor in Rome wanted to send a message to a far-flung corner of his empire like Judea, he did not pick up a telephone or send an email message to his ambassador. Instead, he had to send his instructions by hand, and this could be a hazardous business. The messenger could be intercepted and robbed – or (as often happened) he could turn out to be a crook, and just disappear. Or he might be shipwrecked, or caught up in civil war some-where along the route. The emperor Caligula once sent orders to Jerusalem for his own statue to be put up in the Temple there. This was a particularly risky thing to do, for not only did the Jews dislike the Romans, but they also had no time for artists and sculptors, believing their work to be contrary to the Jewish faith. But while the emperor's instructions were in tran-sit, Caligula was assassinated – and a second ship that left Rome much later with that piece of news arrived in Palestine twenty-seven days earlier than the first one! It was just as well, for if the statue had ever gone up in the Temple, it would cer-tainly have led to civil war, or worse.

The Roman empire, however, was one of the later cultures in which the characters of the Bible were at home. Its earliest sto-ries relate to a world even more ancient than that, going right back to the Stone Age. For not only does the Bible contain many different types of literature, it also covers an enormous time-span. We today are about 2,000 years distant from the most recent events reported in the pages of the New

Testament, but to discover the life setting of the earliest Bible stories, we have to go back by the same length of time again, to the world of 4,000 years ago. This was the setting in which the Old Testament places the stories of Abraham and his family. It was a world so very different from our own that the wheel was a recent invention, and the discovery of iron was yet to come in the future. Abraham himself had a nomadic lifestyle, moving about from place to place in the ancient Middle East. That much at least is not too different from the traditional way of life of modern Arab Bedouin, moving through the desert sands with their camels and herds, and setting up camp where water is to be found. Nowadays, the Bedouin chief is likely to have a limousine as well as a camel, and the fertile desert oasis is likely to have an oil well and other modern comforts, in addition to the all-important supply of fresh water. But in other respects, little has changed. The extended family, the strong sense of community, self-conscious morality, respect for elders – and family feuds – are all ingredients in the early stories of Genesis, just as they would be in any desert encampment today. Nor has the essential power structure of the region changed much. The modern visitor to the Middle East soon senses that politics is all-important here, and being on the right side at the right time can quite literally mean the difference between life and death. Things were just the same through the whole of the Old Testament period. The Old Testament story centres on a neatly defined geographical area – the Fertile Crescent – referred to as 'fertile' because of the fact that all else around was barren wilderness, and a 'crescent' because this expanse of fertile land swept round in an area the shape of the new moon that stretched from the Persian Gulf in the east to Egypt and the river Nile in the west. Each end of this Fertile Crescent was home for a superpower. At the eastern end was the ancient city of Babylon, which saw a succession of civilizations come and go – but always as a world leader. At the other end was the longer-lasting culture of ancient Egypt. In between the two was Palestine, home to a dozen or more smaller states – including Israel and Judah – whose territory was the backyard in which the great powers regularly threw their weight about. The only wise strategy for the inhabitants of these places was to make sure that they were supporting whichever one had the upper hand at any given time.

Both these superpowers exercised an enormous influence on the culture and way of life of the peoples of Palestine and Syria. Long before the emergence of any dateable Bible character, the Sumerians had a great civilisation based in ancient Mesopotamia, much of which is documented in archives and inscriptions that have been unearthed by the work of archaeologists. By the time Hammurabi became king of Babylon in 1792 BC, the city was not only an important political centre, but stood at the heart of an expanding world of culture and learning.

The story of Abraham begins in Ur, not far from Babylon, and Bible readers have often wondered if any of the Old Testament characters ever came into contact either with Hammurabi or his predecessors. Because of the nature of the Bible stories, repeated and retold over many generations, it is impossible to answer that kind of question. But there is no doubt that the influence of a king like Hammurabi spread far and wide, and the basic principles of justice established in Babylon at this period seem to have been adopted in many parts of the Fertile Crescent. That included Israel too, for several elements of the Old Testament case law reflect procedures that were established and widely practised long before any date that can be assigned to even the earliest sections of Israelite law. Some investigators have also claimed to be able to find references to legal principles of the day in certain of the stories concerning Abraham. His ready acceptance of Hagar as a sexual partner when his wife Sarah proved to be childless is one such example. According to texts found at the Mesopotamian city of Nuzu, this was a regular practice of the day, and was specifically built into many marriage contracts. Of course, it is unlikely that the stories of Abraham's family had any direct connections with Nuzu, and even if they did it would be difficult to prove such a thing beyond reasonable doubt. But knowledge of facts like this can obviously help us to set such stories in a plausible historical setting – and therefore understand more clearly their real meaning, in their own day, as well as for ours.

Israel's history never stood still. Things were constantly changing in this ancient world, and the Bible stories reflect this. Not long after Abraham's time, it was the other super-power – Egypt – that took centre stage, at least so far as Israel was concerned. Enforced slavery in Egypt was followed by the amazing escape of a band of dispossessed slaves – led by Moses, under God's guidance, into a new homeland and a new life. Not surprisingly, knowing about Egyptian culture can shed light on some aspects of all that as well. Though it is not always very easy to put what we know of Egypt into a coherent relationship with the traditional stories of the Bible, it has been possible to draw several conclusions about when the exodus might have taken place, and what the circumstances both in Egypt and the Sinai desert – not to mention Canaan – would have been at that time.

One thing we do know for certain is that during this period Egypt was the dominant power in Palestine, and there was nothing remotely like a national Canaanite government, but instead a series of separate city-states, each with its own king. This situation provides the background to the stories contained in the books of Joshua and Judges, and helps to explain why the Israelite tribes needed to deal with one city at a time – for each had a different ruler. The social and economic circumstances which allowed Israel to emerge as the dominant power in this land were highly complex. But one reason why Israel found it so easy was undoubtedly connected with the generally harsh and authoritarian style adopted by these local kings. In the Canaanite city states, real power was concentrated in the hands of only a few people, while the rest worked to maintain them in their positions of privilege. It is not hard to understand how not only the lands, but also the hearts and minds of people would be won over by the rather different concept of society that the emerging nation of Israel brought with it. They regarded God as their only true king, and that meant no one person had any right to claim a position of superiority: everyone was of equal importance, regardless of their social or ethnic origins. In particular, every family had a right to its own parcel of land.

Inevitably, such a view was placed under overbearing pressure right from the outset. 'To be like the Canaanites' was a constant temptation – and when later a king was appointed, there was a good deal of debate about the nature of his power in relation to these basic social ideals of Israel's faith. By the time of Solomon, things had reached breaking point. Politically, he was unquestionably Israel's greatest king, and succeeded in putting his nation on the international map of the day – but at the cost of freedom and equality for its citizens. The tensions this introduced inevitably led to the disintegration of national institutions, as the northern part of the country formed its own state (Israel), leaving only the city of Jerusalem and a small surrounding area as the much smaller kingdom of Judah. But it was not just divergent political theories that led to this collapse. It was the result of intense competition between two incompatible religious systems. On the one hand was the faith stemming from the exodus and the giving of the law at Mount Sinai, and on the other was the traditional religion of the land of Canaan, encountered most frequently in the Old Testament in the figure of the god Baal. Much of the Bible story is taken up with the changing religious allegiances of the people, as they adopt first one and then the other.

A good deal of light has been shed on the worship of Baal by a remarkable archaeological discovery made at a site in Syria, where the ancient Canaanite city of Ugarit flourished in the fifteenth and fourteenth centuries BC. A series of clay tablets contain traditional stories of the doings of Baal and other Canaanite gods and goddesses, and help us to appreciate why they held such a fascination for ancient Israel. Nowadays, religious worship is often peripheral to the real business of everyday life, at least in the Western world. But there was no such possibility of a separation in the ancient world, any more than there would be in traditional Islamic cultures in today's world. In Palestine, everything depended on agriculture, and a key necessity was to ensure that the rains would come at the proper time to ensure the continued fertility of the fields. It was the most natural thing in the world to identify this life-giving water with the activity of the gods, and on occasions the deities themselves might even be identified with the phenomena of the natural world. This meant that a farmer's choice of gods was crucial for survival. Put simply, to be successful it was necessary to worship a god who knew how to grow crops! Now the God of Israel undoubtedly knew how to guide people through deserts: if nothing else, the experiences of Abraham's family, and later of the exodus, had demonstrated that in dramatic fashion. But could the God of these stories grow crops? No one could be certain – and since there were other deities in Canaan, who had apparently been successful at doing this for centuries, was it worth taking the risk? Many thought not, and adopted Canaanite worship as the best way to be sure. The prophets could see the dangers in all this. They asked how a God who had stepped into real events could ever be identified merely with the forces of nature. And they argued forcefully that any kind of worthwhile faith must consist of much more than the perfunctory performance of rituals in a shrine, and must embrace social and moral principles of the kind now found in passages such as the Ten Commandments.

Much of the later Old Testament story is taken up with a tale of inept leadership and spiritual blindness, as first the Assyrians, then the Babylonians, took on the role of political overlord in Palestine. At first sight, leadership and spirituality may not seem to be related. But knowledge of Assyrian and Babylonian practices tells us that religious faith and political allegiance were but different sides of the same coin in those far-off days, and the external symbols of the power of the state were often enshrined in its religious practices. So when Ahaz, the eighth century BC king of Judah, forged an allegiance with the Assyrians, as well as paying taxes to them he also had to install their religious symbols in the Temple of Jerusalem – an action that brought condemnation from the prophet Isaiah. Later, when his son and successor Hezekiah was trying to loosen his ties with Assyria, the first thing he did was to reform the worship of the Temple, getting rid of the signs of submission that his father had placed there. The close intermingling of renewed religious fervour with nationalism is by no means a modern phenomenon. It was these pressures that eventually led to the downfall of both Israel and Judah – Israel succumbing to the Assyrians in 721 BC, and Judah to the Babylonians 135 years later. But it is our knowledge of the total context in which these events took place that enables us to understand it so clearly. Once the Old Testament is placed in its own world, much of what might otherwise be a jumbled jigsaw begins to fall into place.

The final scenes of the Old Testament story were played out against the background of the Persian, and eventually the Greek empires. We need not recount these events here, as we have already looked at them briefly in a previous chapter. But the Greek empire of the fourth century BC genius Alexander the Great, and his successors, set the scene for the world of the New Testament. That world was dominated by the Romans, who by the time of Jesus had established themselves as the empire that would end all empires in the ancient world. By a mixture of military brilliance and ruthless cruelty, they had brought the whole of the Mediterranean world – and more besides – under their control. When Jesus was born, the event had to be dated with reference to the emperor who ruled in Rome (Luke 2:1), and throughout his life, Jesus was constantly in contact with the symbols of Roman imperial power – from the coins bearing Caesar's head, to the tax-gatherers whose crafty intelligence network played an important role in the ruling of the empire.

You might imagine that in such a world there would be even less scope for innovation. Those who succeeded would be the ones who either collaborated with the Romans, or who managed to keep out of sight of the authorities altogether. Jesus found that impossible – and paid the price. But his followers were no less bold, and though some of them too were put to death for their belief in Jesus, their mission was accompanied by remarkable success. As individuals, they had nothing at all going for them. Though Galilee was a great centre of Greek culture, Jesus' original disciples seem not to have been a part of that, but were rural country dwellers. They were people with only limited educational opportunities, who spoke with a strong local dialect (Mark 14:70), and could plausibly be described as 'ignorant and uneducated' (Acts 4:13). They had no great resources behind them, and no multinational corporation to sponsor their work. Yet within less than twenty years of their remarkable experiences of the Holy Spirit on the Day of Pentecost, they had taken the message of Jesus to all parts of the known world, and there were thriving congregations of Christian believers in every major city of the Roman empire.

Though the secret of their success can ultimately be traced to their commitment and life-changing encounters with God's Spirit, when we place their evangelistic programme alongside what we know of life in the Roman empire at the time, it is obvious that they also had a carefully conceived strategy for evangelism. Towards the end of the first century AD, the writer of the book of Revelation observed that God had 'opened a door' in front of them (Revelation 3:8). They went through it without hesitation, for a number of factors came together to make it relatively straightforward (though never easy) for them to share the message of Jesus.

For one thing, there was a common language spoken everywhere. Alexander the Great had been an absolute fanatic for his own native culture, and insisted that the only proper way for civilized people to speak was in his own tongue, which was Greek. By the time of Jesus, it was understood everywhere. This means that Christians could travel anywhere in the empire and make themselves easily understood. It also meant that any literature they produced had an immense potential readership. They exploited all this to the full. Indeed, they were trend setters in the use of new technology, for it was the early Christians who seem to have invented the book as we know it, with sheets of papyrus folded and stitched down the middle to make pages that could easily be opened. Prior to this, much more cumbersome bindings had been in common use.

Something else the Romans worked hard for was to set up a comprehensive system of communications between the main centres of population in their empire. All roads literally led to Rome – and many other cities besides. When we trace Paul's extensive journeys on a map, it is obvious that he was following the major Roman trading routes. All the places he visited were large population centres, and he reckoned that if he could establish growing churches in these, then their members would in turn reach out to their own surrounding provinces. It was a strategy that clearly worked: Paul never went to Colossae, for example, but one of his converts in Ephesus planted a church there too.

Another key to the success of the early Christians is to be found in the fact that there were already significant Jewish communities established throughout the Roman empire. Here in the regular worship of the synagogues, fervent and often fanatical groups met to study the Hebrew scriptures, and to wonder if the promises of the coming of a Messiah to inaugurate God's kingdom would ever be fulfilled. These were exactly the questions to which the earliest followers of Jesus believed they had the answer – and so they headed straight for the synagogue, before tackling other elements of the population whose questions were rather different. Some of these people would be found in the various public lecture halls that were part of the furniture of any city in the Roman empire – and more than once we catch a glimpse of Paul sharing the gospel in just such places (Acts 17:19,20; 19:9,10).

Understanding the nature of Roman society can provide us with a distinctive perception of the success in evangelism that was enjoyed by the early Christians. If we read the New Testament in isolation from its context at this point, we will miss some of the most fundamental lessons to be learned from it. But by seeing how the apostles set about relating the gospel to their own culture, we can gain insights which are invaluable as we face the challenge of doing the same in the rather different world of today.

The same is true in relation to understanding the New Testament books. More than half of them are letters. They have traditionally been called 'epistles', though in the ancient world letters and epistles were not strictly the same thing as each other. We are all familiar with letter writing, and most of us only do it if we have absolutely no alternative. But we all write enough of them to know that you compose a rather different sort of letter depending on whether the recipient is a close friend or the bank manager. I remember spending much time in primary school trying to grasp the difference between a letter that ends 'Yours sincerely' and one that concludes with 'Yours faithfully'. One was supposed to be used for more formal letters, and the other in writing to friends, though if I'm writing to someone I know really well, I don't normally use either of those anyway. Such formalities, though, were just as common in the Roman empire. As we look at ancient letters, it is possible to tell what sort of letters they were just by noting such characteristics. But the Roman world had the 'epistle' as well. Not everybody knew how to write epistles, or would ever need to do so, for this was a more up-market form of communication, much loved by philosophers and poets and other reflective thinkers. If you wanted to set out your ideas on some great political or moral issue of the day, it was quite common to do so in the form of an imaginary letter – apparently addressed to a person, but not really written in personal form, and intended for widespread publication and debate. Modern writers still occasionally use the same general idea. When C S Lewis wanted to write a book on the problem of evil, he realised that no one would buy it if it was a deeply philosophical abstract discourse. Instead, he wrote it as a series of imaginary letters to and from various demons and devils, called it *The Screwtape Letters* – and it became a bestseller. None of his readers ever imagined it was a real correspondence: it was a literary device, chosen to give interest to what might otherwise have been a very dull subject.

What sort of letters did Paul write? Were they 'epistles' – theological tracts dressed up to look like letters – or were they real letters, written to real people? And if they were real letters, what kind of real letters were they? The formal sort you might write to the bank manager, or the more relaxed style in which you would write to your friend? Thanks to a large quantity of ancient letters, found mostly in Egypt, we can without hesitation say that Paul's letters were definitely *not* literary 'epistles', nor were they formal business letters: they were rather the sort of note you would write to a close friend. Many thousands of Greek letters, written on papyrus, show this quite clearly. The English word 'paper' comes from 'papyrus', and this was a sheet of writing material made from the stalks of the papyrus plant, which grew in profusion along the banks of the river Nile in Egypt. A perennial plant, it can reach as much as five metres in height, and was harvested once a year. Parts of the stalk were considered a delicacy to eat, but most of it would be cut up into thin strips, which were then compressed and glued together to form a writing surface. Modern visitors to the Ragab Papyrus Institute in Cairo can still see sheets being manufactured by the same ancient methods. The material it produced was easy to write on, and relatively durable – unless it got damp, in which case mould and mildew would soon destroy it. This is why most of the ancient papyrus documents known to us today originated in Egypt, for the hot desert sands there were the ideal medium in which they could be preserved intact over the centuries.

In these letters, we see an extraordinary kaleidoscope of everyday life in the ancient world: invoices and receipts from the markets, letters from soldiers away from home in foreign parts, love letters, letters to and from parents and children. They preserve a complete cross-section of life, and by comparing the New Testament letters with these, it is obvious that this is where they belong. When Paul wrote to Corinth, or Philippi, or to Philemon, he was writing informal letters to his friends, often in reply to letters they had sent to him. This discovery has a far-reaching impact on the way we should read the letters of the New Testament. Had they been literary epistles, then we would expect them to be carefully measured pronouncements on the great issues that their writers felt to be important. But as letters between friends, we come to them with quite different assumptions. For one thing, we can appreciate that they are a two-way communication – yet we now have access to only one side of this process. Reading them is therefore like listening to one half of a phone conversation. While it is relatively simple to catch the general drift of what is being said, a more detailed understanding requires a certain amount of imaginative reading between the lines. In addition, a person's emotions tend to come through in a letter to friends, whereas in a more formal epistle a writer would be inclined to disguise his or her feelings. Paul's letters inform their readers in no uncertain terms of how he was feeling as he wrote. Joy, anger, and a good deal of humour are all there. When you're writing a very emotional letter – like Galatians or 1 and 2 Corinthians – you are quite likely to say things that you would leave unsaid in calmer moments. You might even find that you've overemphasised this or that point, precisely because you're involved in an argument – and had you been writing in a more detached way, you would have chosen your words more precisely. This is characteristic of Paul too. For example, compare what he says about the Jewish Law in Galatians with his later statements in Romans, or take a look at his unexpectedly earthy advice to those nuisances who were trying to persuade the Christians of Galatia that they needed to get themselves circumcised. He asks why they are only concerned with cutting off little bits of their bodies. 'Why don't they just do a thorough job,' he asks, 'castrate themselves – cut the whole lot off – and be done with it once and for all?' (Galatians 5:12). That may not be exactly the impression most of us have of a writer of the Bible, but in the context of a real letter, written in the heat of an angry debate, doesn't it bring Paul down to earth and help us identify more closely with what he has to say? Yet without the papyrus letters, we might still be thinking of his writings as 'epistles' – and in the process, missing out on much of the immediacy of his advice to those who would follow Jesus.

Clearly, an understanding of the Bible's world can be of enormous help. To appreciate the Bible in its real life context will bring it alive in new ways, and help us to see that its message is not really at home in dusty sanctuaries, but in the hurly-burly of everyday living.

In the first chapter of this book, I shared the story of how my own thinking was challenged when, as a teenager, I first began to read the Bible in a serious way. But it was not just reading the Bible itself that challenged my life – it was reading it through the spectacles of its own times, and seeing how its message arose not as abstract theological speculations about God, but as answers to the questions of people who were desperately searching for spiritual reality and meaning in their life. It was not long after my interest in the Bible was aroused that (for the first time in my school career, I think) I won a class prize, and had to go to the local bookshop to select an appropriate volume. After being lectured in school on what would be considered an 'appropriate' book, I headed for the designated store, only to discover that they stocked no other sort of publication but 'appropriate' books. What is more, they had a very limited stock even of those. At the time I was living in an industrial town in the north of England, which had quite definitely seen better days, and bookshops were not a high priority for the community. This one was a particularly awesome and ancient bookshop, staffed by men in threadbare suits who could themselves have stepped right out of the pages of a Dickens first edition, and where it seemed a transgression of the most serious nature even to open the cover of a book to inspect it before purchase. So I was relieved when I saw that the shelf headed 'religion' was near the door, convenient for a rapid exit back to the relative normality of the street outside. The majority of the stock that seemed to qualify as 'religion' consisted of a collection of antiquated-looking Bibles and hymn books. In this company, just one book caught my eye, though that too had a decidedly sad air to it, smothered by what seemed like fully half an inch of dust. But at least it had a photograph on the dust jacket. It turned out to be a well-known book first written by the German journalist Werner Keller in 1956, and subsequently revised many times. *The Bible as History* was its title, and when I presented it at the counter the manager took one look at it, blew the dust off in a pretentious way, and observed dryly that since it had obviously been in stock for some time I could have it for half price. It is the only time in my life I can recall wanting to refuse a bargain – for if I took it at a knock-down price, that meant there would be some of my prize money left over, and so I had to venture further into the murky depths of the wretched shop and begin my search all over again. My supplementary choice was a book on Queen Victoria, which I suspect I never even opened before it was unceremoniously dumped.

But my other purchase filled me with excitement, as passage after passage opened my eyes to a new world of Bible understanding that I had never even dreamed of. It was certainly quite different from what my experiences of the church had led me to suppose the Bible was all about, and reading and rereading it as a teenager was literally like scales falling from my eyes. I later came to realize that this particular book had its weaknesses as well as strengths, and perhaps rather more of the former than the latter. But in any case, understanding of the ancient world has come a long way in the last fifty years, and there are now many excellent and reliable books available to help readers grasp the realities of the Bible's world.

Inevitably, it has not been possible to embark on anything more than a whirlwind tour of the Bible's world in this chapter, and those who wish to follow through on it ought to consult the various Bible handbooks and encyclopaedias or, for more detailed information on specific texts, dip into Bible commentaries. But I hope it has helped to open up the possibilities that are available when once we begin to read the Bible in its own context. For that is an important step in the endeavour to see what it might mean in our different context. That is where we must now head in the remaining chapters.

## Chapter 4

# Difficulties en route

If you mention the Bible to the average person in the street, especially in Britain, the first thing they will say is likely to be connected to what they regard as difficulties with it. 'Hasn't science disproved it all anyway?' someone will ask – generally someone with no clear understanding of either science or the Bible! Others will observe that the Bible seems to have caused many conflicts in human history, from the Crusades and the Inquisition through to the tragedy of the divided communities in the north of Ireland – and any book that has that sort of effect can hardly be good news. In any case, we might be asked, is the Bible not the source of a lot of prejudice against already hard-pressed minorities? Racism, the sexual exploitation of women, homophobia and similar attitudes have all at one time or another been promoted by people who claimed to be acting on the authority of the Bible. So who wants a book of that sort?

In addition to questions like that, others are likely to be concerned by the fact that it actually seems to contradict itself. Just exactly where *did* Cain get his wife from, if his parents and his brother were the only other people around at the time? Who was it that took Joseph off to slavery in Egypt – the Ishmaelites (Genesis 37:25–27), or a band of Midianites (Genesis 37:28–36)? And who could really claim to know what Amnon said to Tamar as he raped her, when no one else was there (2 Samuel 13:1–21)?

Most of us will have come across these questions, and many others like them. The fact is that the Bible does raise many unsolved problems, and if we deny their existence, or try and sweep them away out of sight, we do ourselves a disservice. If Christians want to get to the bottom of the Bible for themselves, and to communicate its message in an effective way to other people, then we need to face squarely the sorts of questions that ordinary people want to ask about it. Of course, we also ought to be aware of the type of mindset that focuses exclusively on the problems, and makes them in effect an excuse for not taking the Bible's message seriously at all. US novelist Mark Twain once wrote, 'It ain't those parts of the Bible that I can't understand that bother me, it's the parts I do understand.' Many of us today are like that. We can see well enough the point of Jesus' Sermon on the Mount, with its clear statements about loving enemies and turning the other cheek. We have no difficulty at all with his teaching about loving God and loving our neighbour – and when we read of prophets like Amos denouncing injustice and exploitation in the name of God, we can readily identify what they are talking about. The problem often is that we don't want to take them seriously and do anything about it in our own lives. So we must put this matter in proper perspective. For every sentence in the Bible that is difficult to understand, there will be at least a dozen others that we can easily make sense of. When you consider how the Bible came into existence, that in itself is quite remarkable. With sixty-six quite separate writings, produced by many different authors over a period of around a thousand years, and reflecting the influence and lifestyle of many different cultures, it may be considered surprising that *any* of it makes sense to modern readers without some long and involved process of interpretation. If you were to compare the Bible with other works of similar age and antiquity, the difference becomes all the more impressive.

Many of the most striking parts of it can be understood by anyone, with no special knowledge or training at all. The stories that Jesus told certainly fall into this category. In Luke 15, for instance, there are three stories of lost things: a lost sheep, a lost coin, and a lost son – something that everyone can identify with, because they deal with experiences which are familiar to us all. As life has become ever more complex, the awareness of being lost has become one of the human race's greatest challenges. Seneca, a near-contemporary of Jesus himself, observed: 'All my life I have been seeking to climb out of the pit of my besetting sin and I cannot do it and I never will...' Two thousand years later, Ernest Hemingway wrote: 'I live in a vacuum that is as lonely as a radio tube when the batteries are dead, and there is no current to plug in to.' It is little wonder that the teaching of Jesus still speaks to us across the centuries, for he addressed himself to spiritual needs that are part and parcel of what it means to be human. There is not a person alive who has not at some time felt the anguish expressed by Shakespeare's Hamlet when he complained that 'The time is out of joint; O cursed spite, That ever I was born to set it right!' Many people feel that they have been born at the wrong time and place, struggling with apparently impenetrable barriers between themselves and the world, and living a lonely and isolated existence in which meaningful communication with other people gets harder all the time. For people in today's world, when Jesus speaks of lostness we know exactly what he means, and those with the courage and honesty to admit it can see that his answer to our predicament makes good sense.

The same is true of other parables, such as the story of the Good Samaritan (Luke 10:25–37). This presents a different sort of challenge, for we may not grasp all the hidden meanings here unless we have some idea of what Jews and Samaritans thought about each other at the time. But anyone can read it and see what our duty to others should be. More surprisingly, perhaps, we can read many parts of the Old Testament and see what it means without any further effort at interpretation or reflection. The book of Amos, with its perceptive comments on the issues of human rights, needs little further explanation, while the same prophet's denunciation of economic and social exploitation rings bells with people living in many different countries throughout today's world, including those who find themselves at the bottom of the pile in Western democracies.

We could go on, for these and other Bible passages are not restricted by the cultural contexts in which they were first written. They are more like the works of a great artist, with a correspondingly timeless quality about them that we can all appreciate. They deal with where we are – where the human race has always been – our basic needs, feelings and emotions – and their meaning and challenge are obvious as we read them.

To readers who are on the fringes of the Christian church, or who are hesitant believers, puzzled by the apparent problem-passages of the Bible, the message is clear: we should not make too much out of the unresolved questions, but think first of those bits (the majority) that are perfectly clear, and reflect on what God might be saying through them. For many Christians, though, the dilemma is rather different. We have become so defensive about our faith, and the Bible as one of the foundational elements of that faith, that we are often tempted to ignore or play down the very real questions that it sometimes raises for other people. It is perfectly easy to understand why we should do this, for if we ourselves have found a life-giving message within its pages, we naturally want to be positive about it, and if we have committed our own lives to what we find in the Bible, then there are certain mechanics of self-preservation that will tend to resist and shut out questioning or critical comments. From that perspective, it is all too easy to minimize the differences between ourselves and the world of the Bible. It is easy to gloss over things with glib statements about human nature being the same today as it was back then. In one sense, that is all true of course, and the fundamental problem of the human race has not changed: we are struggling to make sense of things in a world where we seem to be alienated from creation and from other people just as much as we are separated from God. But recognising that does not by itself break down the barriers of time, place and culture that still stand between us and the people of whom the Bible speaks.

While most of Jesus' teaching is perfectly clear without any further explanation, some parts of it do take for granted an outlook on life and a social situation that most of us know nothing about. For example, in common with other Bible writers, Jesus regularly uses pictures taken from farming, and to understand the point he is making it might be necessary to have some appreciation of the background. So how much do you know about growing grapes? Unless you know something, you are certain to have a problem with the teaching in John 15:1–10, where Jesus says that the relationship between himself and his followers is like the way a grapevine grows. At one crucial point, he says something about vines that could never happen in a real vineyard – and in doing so he highlights the key teaching of the parable in the most striking way possible. Look at the passage yourself, and see if you can spot it. (If you need a hint, look at verse 6). Then there are other parts of the Bible that presuppose an understanding of things that are not just foreign to our own expectations, but may actually be abhorrent to us. Sacrifice is a good example here. All of the Old Testament books take this for granted as part and parcel not only of religious worship, but of daily life too. Moreover, several of them are exclusively taken up with explaining in all the gory details exactly how sacrificial procedures should be carried out. This is certainly light years away from the life experience of Western people today. Christians might sing about sacrifice with enthusiasm in the familiar, disinfected words of hymns, but the vast majority of us have neither seen a sacrifice offered, nor can we really imagine what it must have been like. In addition, most of us would find the gratuitous death of animals in the name of religious worship a thoroughly shameful thing. Like many other aspects of the Bible, an issue like this also needs to be placed in perspective, and we should remember that this type of worship is typical not just of ancient Israel, but of many cultures around the world even today. Even so, it is difficult to work up much enthusiasm for Bible passages that sometimes read like a handbook for the operations of a butcher's shop – which, of course, is what the Temple in Jerusalem often was. As well as those activities which we would be inclined to classify as 'religious', people would also on occasion meet there for a meal with their friends. At a later date, when Paul was writing to the Christians in the Greek city of Corinth, he highlighted exactly the same feature in relation to the temples there which were dedicated to traditional Greek and Roman deities.

This is where the sort of information we looked at in chapter 3 can be of some assistance to us. We may still find ourselves mentally and emotionally turned off by some aspects of life in the Bible's world, but at least if we can begin to understand what it was like, and why these people thought as they did, then we can begin to take whatever insights they had and apply them to our own rather different situation today. Even that, though, can have its dangers. Some of the books written by experts on the Bible can easily create the impression that without a degree in ancient history you have no chance of ever understanding it. In reality, most of us are not too concerned to know what the Bible might have meant back then to its original readers: we want to know what it might mean now for us, living in a very different world indeed. To major on its ancient origins can easily exclude consideration of the very questions that today's people – both Christians and unbelievers – want answers to. Traditionally, those two different sorts of questions have been answered by different types of experts: the former by those who make a specialised study of the Bible, and the latter by experts in systematic theology. In this respect, the church has simply adopted the excessive reverence for 'experts' that has become widespread in everyday life, where people often seem to be learning more and more about less and less. In the face of this, the average Christian reader might easily be tempted to conclude that it is impossible for an ordinary person to make sense of the Bible, and it should therefore be left to the experts to tell us whatever they think we might need to know.

Back in the 1970s I wrote a dissertation for a PhD degree at the University of Manchester. The subject on which I wrote was Paul – in particular Romans, Galatians and 1 Corinthians – and his relationship with various mystical and speculative sectarian spiritual movements in the world of his day. My thesis was a heavily academic tome, as was appropriate for the purpose for which it was written. But I had always been impressed by the way in which my understanding of Paul was constantly enriched not so much by the erudition of other scholars, as by my daily experience of life as a church leader. One of the particularly challenging aspects of obtaining a doctorate from Manchester was that at that university one's dissertation had to be subjected to an examination which took place in public – which meant that it was not only your academic advisers, but all your friends as well who discovered what you didn't know. I remember returning home in the autumn of 1972, after successfully defending my work in this rather formidable atmosphere, ready to put my feet up for a few years and recover from what at the time seemed to have been an almost superhuman effort. My wife Olive, however, had other ideas. 'Now you've proved that you know what Paul's all about', she said, 'you should write a book to tell the rest of us.' In due course, the book was published, illustrated and given a glossy cover – and was an enormous success. In fact, it is still in print more than a quarter of a century later, and has been translated into almost thirty different languages. The only people who never liked it were a handful of crusty reviewers, who observed not only that the book was full of pictures, but also that I had ditched all their favourite jargon. They searched in vain for a single use of such words as 'justification', 'propitiation', and the like – and pronounced that a book on Paul without these magic words was totally worthless. I knew then that I had achieved my goal, for I was quite certain that what Paul *meant* by all those words was expressed perfectly clearly, and the absence of mystifying jargon was a definite plus – something with which hundreds of thousands of readers all around the world have obviously agreed.

Though the Bible demands our serious attention, you do not need to be an expert in either ancient history or language – or modern theological mumbo-jumbo – in order to understand its message and apply it to your life. My childhood experiences of the church warned me off that temptation right from the start. One of my most vivid memories of the church I attended as a child is of a large picture that hung in one of the small rooms, out of sight of the casual visitor, but which I perused in detail Sunday after Sunday for several years, as my Sunday School teacher sat below it. Whether he realised at the time that most of my attention was fixed not on him but on the picture, I do not know. It was a painting of the tent of worship (tabernacle) used in the desert by the Israelite tribes while in transit from Egypt to the promised land of Canaan. The artist had obviously gone to great lengths to analyse the Old Testament books of Numbers and Leviticus, to ensure that all the details were as correct as they could be. To a bored child, it was an impressive sight, with the curtains of the tent in different materials and colours, and the cloud of God's presence boldly stretched out from sandy earth up to sky-blue heaven. It had so much detail there was always something new to notice, with the priests going about their duties, or the tribes camped in symmetrical blocks around the central structure, each one identified by a triangular pennant, as if they were attending a 1920s Boy Scouts Jamboree. But it was not just an interesting picture. It became to me a symbol of a whole way of looking at the Bible, for in the church circles in which I was raised, detailed knowledge of the tabernacle and all its contents was considered an intellectual accomplishment to be highly desired. In the course of a typical year there would always be at least one visiting preacher who would come with models and maps of this ancient structure, to enlighten the congregation about its meaning. I dare say one or two of them did occasionally read other passages of scripture, but if so I never heard them speak of it. Above all else, knowledge of these obscure parts of the Old Testament was revered as a sure sign of immense spirituality.

I could continue with personal reminiscences, but the point is this: God does not call us to be Christians in order that we might first be ancient historians. It is all too easy for us to get ourselves locked into a time warp, so that we know – and sympathise with – a world that has long since disappeared, while failing either to comprehend or identify with the people amongst whom we actually live. God's kingdom is not about mere intellectual hair-splitting, whether of the kind that would specialise in knowledge of the tabernacle or the rather different – but no less pointless – disputations of many theological experts. People today need to know what the Bible means, in words they can understand and relate to. We must deal with specific problem areas not as a purely academic exercise, but as a means of opening up the Bible's essential message – to allow God to speak to us through its pages. If we lose sight of that, we have lost what is most important.

There will always be tensions when we try to apply more widely the teachings of a book which originated in particular times and places. When Martin Luther discovered God speaking to him through the writings of Paul, he had no doubt of the reality of his experience, for it changed his life. But he had great difficulty relating what he learned from Paul to what he read in other parts of the New Testament. In particular, he could not reconcile what he understood to be Paul's emphasis on salvation as a free gift from God with what other Bible writers – notably James – seemed to say about the importance of doing good in order to please God. By way of resolving this, Luther effectively downgraded James – along with the Old Testament – while promoting Paul to centre stage. He was not the first to think along these lines: the second century heretic Marcion had floated a similar idea, and many influential theologians today would adopt much the same point of view. No doubt this is an extreme solution, and it certainly raises as many problems as it resolves. But even if we do not agree with it, the problem is still there, for how can the Bible's message be reinterpreted for new generations in ways that will not undermine its essential integrity?

This process of reinterpretation began even before all the books of the Bible had been written down. One of the earliest traces of such a concern is found in the messages of the eighth century BC Israelite prophet, Hosea. Faced with the impending collapse of his own culture, he looked around for some explanation of the predicament in which his people found themselves. Why was it that they were God's people, and yet their present existence seemed to convey little of a sense of God's presence? Under God's guidance, Hosea found some clues that would enable him to answer that in the sad circumstances of his own life. Married to a woman called Gomer, Hosea discovered that the maintenance of a stable relationship was no easy matter. The two separated, and in a society where women had little economic leverage, Gomer ended up as a prostitute. She was ultimately rescued from this predicament by Hosea himself – and he saw in his own turbulent marriage, and in his three children, a picture of God's dealings with his people Israel. All his children were given symbolic names, which became a vehicle for the prophet's message to the people. The first of them was called Jezreel – 'because', said Hosea, speaking in the name of God, 'it will not be long before I punish the king of Israel for the murders that his ancestor Jehu committed at Jezreel' (Hosea 1:4). The meaning of this reference to Jehu is clarified by the stories of his exploits contained in 2 Kings 9:30–10:14. They include the barbaric murders of Jezebel, King Ahab's queen, along with large numbers of their other relatives. The book of Kings was not written at the time of Hosea, though we may assume that the stories were well-known in his day, and they were told as part of the heroic story of Israel's past. In that context, Jehu's massacre and bloody coup was seen as a thoroughly good thing – just as Joshua's annihilation of all the inhabitants of Jericho had been a few centuries before. Stories like this are often embarrassing to modern readers of the Bible, especially Christians who are familiar with Jesus' injunctions about loving enemies and turning the other cheek. But Hosea was evidently unhappy with them as well – and declared quite unequivocally that, whatever others may think, behaviour of this sort was contrary to the fundamental moral laws of God's world, and would not go unpunished. Christians today would tend to warm to Hosea's view of things – but let us not forget that he was, in effect, reinterpreting some aspects of the Bible's story in order to apply it the more effectively to the changed circumstances of his own day.

We can see the same process of reinterpretation and application behind the various history books of the Old Testament. It seems likely that the great epic story contained in Joshua to 2 Kings was compiled at the time when Jerusalem had been overthrown by the Babylonians, and many of its inhabitants were taken into exile in Babylon itself. Of course, the stories were not made up then, and we can be sure that some of them had already existed for many years, and would be widely known. But with a fresh – and potentially terminal – crisis in the nation's life, it was necessary to re-examine the past and apply its lessons to changed circumstances. The facts about the past were well known, and could easily be consulted in various written documents – books with titles like *History of the Kings of*

*Israel, History of the Kings of Judah,* or *The Book of Jashar,* none of which has survived the passage of time. But in order that their stories might continue to be relevant, they needed to be interpreted, viewed from new perspectives, and applied to different situations.

As time passed, the need for such reinterpretation became more urgent. By the time of Jesus, many Jewish thinkers realised that if their Scriptures were not somehow brought up to date and applied to the new challenges of life in the Roman empire, then they were in danger of being lost for ever as a relevant part of the human heritage. It was this concern that explains the arguments between Pharisees and Sadducees in the New Testament period. The Pharisees are often disparaged as having introduced a lot of complex rules and regulations to explain the apparently simple law of the Old Testament. But their intentions were a lot more sophisticated than that. They had no doubt that the Old Testament should be their supreme rule of life and belief. But they also realised that it belonged to a world that had disappeared, and its books had no immediate application to the rather different kind of society in which they now lived. To be relevant it needed to be explained in fresh ways. For example, the Ten Commandments instructed people to keep the Sabbath day holy. But what did that really mean in everyday terms? What, exactly, should people do and not do on the Sabbath day? To answer that, the Pharisees developed their own list of specific actions that people would find relevant to their lifestyle under the Romans. The Sadducees, on the other hand, disallowed this, and had no time for anyone who tried to reinterpret the Old Testament, or apply it in this direct way to their own situation. As a result, they could not accept many of the beliefs of other Jews – and they simply disappeared as an influential group not long after the time of Jesus.

One of the best-known interpreters of the Old Testament at this time was Philo. He was born into a Jewish family in Alexandria in Egypt, some little time before the birth of Jesus. Many of his family became deeply involved in politics, both in Egypt and elsewhere. But Philo was more interested in exploring the thinking of Greek writers and philosophers, especially the Stoics. He found many of their ideas very attractive, but he was also a committed Jew and wanted to preserve his ancestral faith alongside the new insights of the scientists and other thinkers of his day. It was quite a challenge, but he managed it by reading much of the Old Testament as if it was a kind of allegorical or symbolic presentation of the theories of the philosophers. By so doing, he was able to claim that anything Plato had thought of, Moses had articulated several centuries before! Much of his argument is contrived and artificial, but the literary tools with which he drew this conclusion have been used by many Christians ever since. The device he used with most precision was 'typology'. By locating the meaning of the Old Testament events not so much in what happened as in what he thought they meant, he was able to discover therein hidden themes that would certainly have surprised their original authors – but which naturally supported his own view of life with remarkable precision. Such a procedure is open to abuse, for once the text has been cut adrift from its historical setting it is easy to discover all sorts of spurious lessons in it. But that does not discourage many people from trying, even today. The same essential procedure was used by the tabernacle specialists of my youth, to whom I have already referred. The great fascination which this structure held for them had absolutely nothing to do with the nature of Israelite worship between the exodus and the conquest of Canaan. Rather, its importance for them was that they were able to use it as a convenient symbolic vehicle through which to discover their own particular brand of Christian theology in the pages of the Old Testament. It is not my concern here to discuss the legitimacy or otherwise of this procedure – only to observe that even very conservative Christians are evidently willing to admit to certain difficulties with some parts of the Bible. In this instance, they are effectively saying that the stories of Israel's ancient history are of no immediate relevance to Christians as they stand. They need to be made relevant by being transposed into a different theological and cultural key – a key, moreover, which clearly goes far beyond the ways in which the Bible's original writers and readers understood and articulated their experiences of God.

Most people can see that there will inevitably be a degree of discontinuity between the experience of today's Christians and ancient Israelites. At the very least, the technological advances of the past century guarantee that we will have different expectations and understandings of the world than our counterparts three thousand years ago. But are there other, more far-reaching differences that affect the central core of the Bible's message in a more radical and profound way? What about the ancient view of the world, for example? In Bible times, it was taken for granted that the earth was flat, and if you went too near the edge you were quite likely to fall off – not off into outer space, but into a different dimension of existence. The universe was commonly thought of as rather like a big gateau, with three separate layers. The earth on which we live was sandwiched in the middle, between the top layer (heaven) where God is, and the bottom layer (Sheol) where the dead reside. Today we all know that as a matter of fact the world is not made anything like that. The earth itself is not flat, and most Christians would not think of heaven as a place like London or Los Angeles, that could be marked on a map – nor that the world of the dead is an underground cave beneath our feet that might be tunnelled into if we were able to dig deep enough. Space exploration has shown that God's universe is infinitely more complex – and attractive – than that. But many Christians seem to live in a state of spiritual paralysis at this point, afraid to face questions that seem too big to answer. When Yuri Gagarin became the first person to travel in space in 1961, and returned to declare that he had not seen God up there, Christians rightly dismissed his observations as eccentric and naïve, for few people ever thought of God like that anyway. But there is also a more serious side to his statement, for if it is not literally the case that heaven can be reached by spaceship above the clouds, then what do we make of stories like the ascension that seem to presuppose it can? And how should we understand Bible statements about angels and demons, and a thousand and one other details that seem clearly linked to the view that the universe is like a three-tier cake?

There are other circumstances which also underline the very far-reaching difference between our outlook today and the thinking of people in Bible times. If my garden refuses to grow anything next summer, there are several things I might do about it. I can dig it more thoroughly, and incorporate lots of organic material and fertilisers, in the hope that things will get better. If I am really determined to get to the bottom of the problem, I may take samples of soil from different parts of the garden, and have them analysed by a specialist in soil fertility – and then follow the advice I am given. But if I had been a farmer in Bible times, things would have been rather different. I would not instinctively assume that there was something wrong with my agricultural procedures, and then try to correct them. Instead I would be more likely to conclude that something must be wrong with the soil. Perhaps a demon of infertility had taken hold, in which case I would send first for a magician to perform appropriate rituals to make the ground productive again. If I was ill, I would do the same thing, and send for a magician rather than a doctor.

In relation to everyday reading of the Bible, we might well ask whether all this really matters anyway. For example, in Psalm 139 the poet celebrates God's power with these words: 'If I went up to heaven, you would be there; if I lay down in the world of the dead, you would be there' (v 8). The picture evoked by this imagery is clearly that of a three-story universe, with heaven above the sky and the world of the dead (Sheol) under the ground. Even though we no longer share that view of how things are, most readers would not therefore conclude that the passage was irrelevant, but would probably make an automatic mental adjustment. After all, the psalms are poetry, and it is only the worst kind of poetry that deals with language in its most literal meanings. What the poet is getting at is obvious anyway: no matter where anyone might go, however far removed from ordinary civilised life it might seem, God will still be there. But other Bible passages are not so straightforward. Think of the story of King Saul in the Old Testament, who began his reign with such promise but ended up as a deranged maniac, trying to kill everyone he knew. Most readers of these stories would conclude that the unfortunate Saul was suffering from a form of mental illness. Indeed, the stories about his behaviour have often been analysed from that point of view, and though any diagnosis based only on documentary evidence must always be risky, some have concluded that he must have been suffering from a form of schizophrenia. But the people who wrote the Old Testament – in common with all ancient peoples – tended to look for other explanations even of physical illness, and so the Bible reports that he was suffering from the influence of 'an evil spirit' (1 Samuel 16:14–23, 18:10, 19:9). Many people today would be inclined to treat such statements with cynicism. That would certainly not be the first place we would look for an explanation, for we do not, on the whole, think that unseen malevolent forces cause illness. Instead, we would expect it to have a series of physical or mental causes, all of them internal to the sufferer. But if that is true, where does it leave the Bible? Can we remain honest to ourselves, and to our understanding of God, by glossing over such matters? Or should we take the advice of the German theologian Rudolf Bultmann, and admit that such aspects of the Bible's message need to be 'demythologised'? By that, he simply means that we must re-articulate the essential core of the Bible's message in the language and thought patterns of today, rather than sticking with what may be the outmoded and inaccurate assumptions of past ages.

In practice, it is not quite as simple as that. Though Bultmann himself wrote many erudite books explaining what such a demythologised Christianity would look like, other people think that he has simply reproduced what may well be the inaccurate assumptions of his own philosophical background! And quite apart from that, the whole business of this demythologising inevitably raises a further question about just what are the bits of the Bible's message that reflect outmoded assumptions and should now be updated? Where should such updating begin and end – and how much can we adapt without changing the essential nature of the Bible's message? Asking questions like this is – in terms of the history of the human race – a relatively recent phenomenon, and a very Western thing as well. It is only within the last three hundred years that such matters have caused any problems. Before that, people viewed the world in essentially the same terms as the ancients. Even at the time of the Reformation, many people still thought the world was flat, and had an essentially superstitious and magical view of the course of human life. But all that changed in a process that came to be known as the Enlightenment.

Beginning in the seventeenth century – though with its roots even earlier – there was an explosion of knowledge of such enormous proportions that it has fundamentally affected the lives and thinking of every one of us. We all know a little about it, from our history lessons at school if nothing else. For this was the great age of discovery. Quite literally, the map of the world was being redrawn: new lands were discovered and new facts about this planet where we live. Nicolaus Copernicus, the sixteenth century Polish astronomer, had revolutionised scientific thinking about the workings of our world in relation to other planets in the solar system, then a century later Sir Isaac Newton saw an apple fall from a tree and formulated an understanding of how gravity works. Travellers like Christopher Columbus (1451–1506) put new theories to the practical test. Beginning from the premise that the earth was not flat after all, he concluded that it must be possible to sail westwards and reach the east – and less than twenty years after his death, the Portuguese explorer Ferdinand Magellan had succeeded in sailing right around the globe. It is hardly surprising that the immediately succeeding period of history should have been labelled the Enlightenment. For it heralded one of the greatest periods of change the world has ever seen, with breathtaking advances in every sphere of human knowledge. It was indeed like the dawning of a great light where previously there had only been darkness and superstition.

Alongside this great advance in factual knowledge of the world and its workings, there was also a philosophical quest for the meaning of it all. Enlightened people wanted to know where they might find the ultimate truth about the world and its inhabitants. Some of them were convinced that the source of all their new discoveries was God. In his book *Principia*

*Mathematica* (1687), Sir Isaac Newton wrote, 'This most beautiful system of the sun, planets and comets, could only proceed from the counsel and dominion of an intelligent and powerful Being, this Being governing all things... as Lord God.' But others – noticeably philosophers – were not so sure. As they considered their own new discoveries it seemed that they owed their success only to hard thinking and sheer intelligence. It was people – and their brains – who had made such amazing progress. So, they reasoned, people and their brain power must surely be capable of determining the ultimate truth about the universe and human life. Moreover, the 'truth' they had discovered seemed to have little or nothing to do with religious belief. It had not come to them from outside – from God – but from their own reason. So by the nineteenth century popular thought was moving to the conclusion that thinkers, especially scientists, must have the *real* truth about things – and religion, though interesting, had no absolute value that could apply at all times and places and be relevant to the lives of all people. At best, it was a collection of personal opinions; at worst, a superstitious hangover from an unsophisticated past. Many leading Christians went along with all this, especially when they saw that the exponents of scientific investigation were about to turn their attention to the Bible itself. They imagined that once the Bible was read 'like any other book', its authority would somehow disappear. In a mad scramble to avoid that, they were only too eager to assert that the essence of the Bible was not actually about the truth in any ultimate or all-embracing sense, but only about how religious people feel or think about God. As a result, instead of looking to the church to explain the meaning of life (as they had done previously), people began to look to the scientists. Instead of believing in God, they came to believe in atoms and molecules, in stars and galaxies. Scientific and economic theories came to be regarded as the ultimate and absolute truths which alone could explain the workings of the universe.

In this intellectual climate it was inevitable that thinking people should come to the conclusion that the ultimate judge of what is real and imaginary, what is true and false, what makes sense and what is nonsense, should be human reason. The masterminds of the age of Enlightenment concluded that there was nothing that cannot be comprehended in purely rational, common-sense terms, and believed that even the most intractable mysteries about the world and about human life will ultimately be solved by hard thinking. The facts seemed to support such a view, as one field of knowledge after another was transformed as a result of the application of systematic and informed thinking. Science became an exact discipline, not a series of vague speculations. Medical knowledge was revolutionised, as it became obvious that every disease was the result of an identifiable physical cause – and the doors were opened to massive advances in the alleviation of human misery. Speculation and ignorance were swept away almost overnight. But then came the realisation that if the rules of the scientist were absolutely and ultimately true, they must have been so for as far back in history as anyone could look. That meant it must also be possible to make a fresh appraisal of key events in the past. Previously, such things had been known only through the unsophisticated responses of the generations that had gone before, but now it was possible to re-open the books, and ask how things would have looked to modern people in the light of what was considered to be a more perfect understanding of how things work.

The Christian faith – the Bible in particular – was a ready quarry of such ancient materials, apparently just waiting to be reshaped in this way. It was taken for granted that what really happened in the past (as distinct from what the ancients *thought* had happened) must, more or less, have been the same as what people experienced in the eighteenth and nineteenth centuries, and since most people then (andcertainly the intellectual élites) attributed their experiences to the influence of some other world, preferring to look for 'rational' explanations of common occurrences rather than talk of God or the miraculous, this is how things must always have been. Freed from the darkness of the past, such people concluded that they could finally understand the realities behind ancient religious prejudices – and when they got to the bottom of it all using this approach, many events turned out to be nothing like as spectacular or amazing as books like the Bible had led previous generations to believe.

Arguments like this have had a far-reaching effect on modern thinking not only about the Bible, but about the whole meaning of Christian faith. As long ago as the eighteenth century, they sent ripples of dismay through the religious establishments of Europe. In answer to all this, some leading thinkers went so far as to redefine the whole basis of Christian belief. Friedrich Schleiermacher (1768–1834) was one of the most influential theologians of his day, and faced with the prospect of the Bible being exposed to such rationalist thinking, he declared that, though the Bible contains much alleged history, real belief is not dependent on such things being factually true. Not facts, but feelings, he said, are at the heart of Christianity – therefore the core of real faith is not something that can be investigated by human reason. With certain modifications, this view was accepted by most subsequent students of the Bible, so much so that its initiator has been called 'the father of modern theology'. Schleiermacher of course was aware of the facts from which we began in this chapter. He knew well enough that the Bible writers assumed the earth was flat, that the universe was like a giant cake with three tiers, and that in most respects their geographical and scientific knowledge is now outmoded. He genuinely wanted to save the essence of biblical faith from being jettisoned along with the trappings of a bygone age. Unfortunately, his understanding of the 'essence' was determined not by a critical appraisal of the Bible, but by a cool calculation of what was likely to be allowed to slip through the sieve of early nineteenth century rationalism.

But if the Bible's essential message – about God – is true in any absolute way, then it makes no sense at all to link it to the changing fashions of human insights into the workings of the world. The Bible does not claim to be a book about science, or geography – or even history for that matter. It claims to speak about God, and how God relates to our world and to us as people. Naturally, the Bible writers just took for granted the scientific knowledge of their day. They were writing for specific people in particular times and places, and in order to communicate anything at all it was necessary to make certain assumptions that would be recognisable by those for whom they wrote. Pictures of a three-tier universe, descriptions of the nature and course of diseases, and other details were taken for granted as a total part of the picture. These things were not themselves the picture of God which they wished to present: they were nothing more than the frame, in which the canvas was mounted. This is why advances in human knowledge are not in themselves any sort of threat to the Bible and its message. In principle, it ought to have been possible to do as Rudolf Bultmann suggested, and change the forms in which we think about God, while leaving the essential message intact. But it turned out to be a very difficult thing to do. According to the book of Genesis the first, and most far-reaching human failure is that we want to be like God, and make 'God' in our own image. Most of us have an in-built tendency to do just that, defining the sort of God we can believe in by primary reference to our own low-level spiritual experience. So it is important to identify what are the most distinctive features of the Bible's message, in order to ensure that we do not lose it in any process of interpretation.

Christians have been trying for centuries to encapsulate the core of the Bible in just a sentence or two, and it is unlikely that I can succeed where others have failed. But a sentence from John's Gospel will make a good starting point. Writing sometime in the first century AD, John summed up so much of Christian belief by asserting, with deceptive simplicity, that God in the person of Jesus 'became a human being and, full of grace and truth, lived among us' (John 1:14). This affirms that God exists (there is a power and a person greater than ourselves, whose existence is not restricted by the conditions of human life), and that this God has chosen to become involved in the life of our world. God became truly a part of it through Jesus. In other sections of his writings, John goes on to explain in greater detail the nature of God's relationship with those who see things this way, and commit themselves to the style of living and believing demonstrated by Jesus.

When we put all this alongside the assumptions of many people today, we begin to see in clearer focus the precise nature of the questions that the Bible addresses to our culture. For the really awkward question is not about how the world works, or where heaven is, or what shape the earth is. Instead, it is about the meaning of life and the nature of our existence. Does the physical world belong to anybody? Does anyone care about it? Is it going anywhere? Does it have any intrinsic meaning? The answer of eighteenth century physicists was that it is a closed scientific system, operating according to fixed and unchangeable 'laws of nature'. The Bible clearly challenges that. It is not a closed system, it says; it is open to interaction with an all-powerful God who has a deep personal concern for its well-being. Then in relation to human life, we might ask why we are here. In the total context of all history, does my brief existence mean anything? Is life going anywhere – or is it an endless round of pessimism, frustration, and ultimate despair? The materialist viewpoint has little to say to satisfy those deep longings of every human person, that each life should have a meaning. But the Bible holds out hope – hope of a Jesus, who offers a way to personal and corporate fulfilment now, and who puts life in the perspective of something much larger, the kingdom of God and the never-ending life of God in person. Reflecting on the logical outcome of all this, if there really is an all-powerful, loving God who relates directly to this world and its people through Jesus, then at those points where God's life impinges on it, we can expect things to happen that are apparently incapable of rational explanation. By definition, this assumption also challenges the sort of thinking handed down from the Enlightenment, which asserted that things with no rational explanation do not exist.

The real distinctiveness of the Bible is concerned not with the externals of life, but with the meaning of it all. Can anyone help me in the ongoing challenges of life? The scientific materialist must answer: 'No, you're on your own.' But the Bible offers a different kind of answer. Yes, it says, this is God's world and God can be found in it. The ultimate question is who is right about *this* – not what shape is the world, or how does it work?

Put in these terms, it might seem as if this is a purely modern dilemma, created for the reader of the Bible by trends in Western thinking during the last two or three centuries. But the Bible writers themselves were familiar enough with people whose assumptions about life and its meaning were fundamentally different from their own. Even in those allegedly unsophisticated days of the early church, by no means everyone would have agreed that life only made sense in the context of belief in a loving and all-powerful God. Quite the reverse, in fact, for the prevailing philosophy of the first century AD also adopted an essentially mechanistic view of life. There was a widespread sense of alienation from the physical world, as people felt themselves hard-pressed in so many areas and concluded that bodily existence was basically flawed. Plato even wrote of the body as a 'prison' – and the only way out was to look for some escape from the shackles of this-worldly existence, usually by supposing that at death the 'spirit' would break free and find true fulfilment in some other world. Naturally, gods of one sort or another often featured in this analysis of the human predicament – but generally as alien forces, and often they were themselves identified as the source of human misery.

Jesus and his followers clearly challenged this pessimistic view of things. The God of whom they spoke was not remote and unknowable, but accessible to ordinary people. This God was not a celestial robot, programmed to be antagonistic to the earth's inhabitants, but a personal being, whose love for all had been plainly shown in the life, death and resurrection of Jesus. Far from being part of the ancient world and its thinking, Christians have always been distinctive in the way they understood life's possibilities and its ultimate meanings. There was a strong contrast between the Christian view and the view of the prevailing culture long before the Enlightenment took place. It is essentially this same contrast which characterises the Bible's message as it relates to our own situation today.

Of course, much has happened since the heady days of the Enlightenment, when Western thinkers thought they could solve everything by their own unaided efforts. Today, everything seems a good deal less precise than it did at one time. A hundred years ago, some readers of the Bible were quite happy to dismiss its message out of hand, simply because it was the product of an ancient culture – and how could people who lived long ago possibly know more than us? Without the benefits of a modern Western education, it was taken for granted that they must have a defective understanding of things. But we can now see that attitude for what it is – a form of intellectual imperialism that also manifested itself in the political expansion of Western empires into Africa, America and other parts of the non-European world. The idea that Western ways of life and thinking are always best has been exposed as a folly, not least because it has been people motivated by a commitment to the life of reason who have supervised some of the worst atrocities ever seen in human history – including the obscene massacres of the First World War, and the mass murders of the Holocaust in Hitler's Germany. More and more people are asking, If this is what unaided human reason can produce, then why should anybody respect it? The assumption that it is possible for us to know everything has also been questioned by more recent advances in scientific thinking, especially in astrophysics. The old idea that the world is a closed system, and that 'laws of nature' can never change or be overthrown has now been abandoned. To be sure, more often than not things work in predictable ways. But the discovery of black holes, quasars and other astronomical phenomena has introduced a dimension of the unknown – even the Unknowable – into the neatly self-contained systems of Enlightenment scientists. In the light of such knowledge, the possibility that there is another dimension of existence ('God') which can impinge on life in this earth (in events we call 'miracles') can no longer be denied. Furthermore, this all seems to tie in with the experience of many people today.

Not long ago I went to the hairdresser. It was one of those days when I had a lot to do, with many engagements. I was looking forward to a quiet hour at the hairdressers. Imagine my surprise, then, when the first thing he asked me was what I thought about the supernatural. It turned out that he, and some of his friends, had experienced some strange things which they were inclined to believe were due to forces from some other spiritual world, beyond the things we can see and handle. The person in question is not a Christian – indeed he is a thoroughly secular, 'modern' fellow – but had no difficulty in supposing that there must be more to life than meets the eye. In the course of our conversation he went on to say that in a previous generation he could have gone to the church for an explanation of what he was experiencing – but, so far as he could see, Christians no longer believe in 'that sort of thing'. What he was saying was that we have become so imbued with a 'scientific' materialist view of the world that we find little or no room in our thinking for a unique and truly 'supernatural' God. Whether we can now do that is perhaps the most awkward question of all that the Bible addresses to us.

Reconciling modern discoveries about the world with the Bible's questions to us is a two-way process. We want to know what difference our modern insights will make as we begin to grapple with the Bible for ourselves today. The answer I have suggested is that they do not need to make so much difference at all, for questions about science and cosmology are not the ultimate concern of the Bible. By all means we need to understand the Bible's claims in the context of its own culture, and then transpose what we find into our own thought world. In one sense, the Bible writers belonged to a more primitive world than ours – though who can truly apply that adjective to the people who built the pyramids, or who established some of the largest empires the world has ever seen? At the same time, the Bible's message was constantly challenging the assumptions even of its own day – assumptions about God, and about the world, and the meaning of life itself. This challenge deals with matters that go far beyond the concerns of scientists or historians, and the questions it poses are as relevant today as ever they were. That is why the most demanding question of all is not one that we address to the Bible, but what the Bible says to us.

## Chapter 5

# Paths to the destination

> O my love's like a red, red rose,
> That's newly sprung in June.

With these words, Robert Burns introduced one of his best-known songs – a song no doubt inspired by his own relationship with a particular woman, and yet penned in such a way that anyone who has ever fallen in love will be able to identify with the sentiments. As the song proceeds, the poet goes on not only to praise his lover's attractive physique; he also declares his own unswerving faithfulness to her – swearing (perhaps rather rashly) that:

> I will love thee still, my dear,
> Till all the seas go dry...
> And the rocks melt in the sun...

We find the same kind of poetry in the Bible. The Song of Solomon is an extended collection of love poems, in which a woman and her partner celebrate their love for each other. In the process, they too use somewhat extravagant language. The woman is described as 'a secret garden, a walled garden, a private spring' (4:12), while at another point her lover avers, 'You are as graceful as a palm-tree, and your breasts are clusters of dates' (7:7).

If we were to take any of these statements (whether from Burns or the Bible) at face value, and understand them according to the literal meaning of their words, these poems would conjure up a rather grotesque image. Was Burns' lover really a flower, red all over? And what sort of identikit picture could you construct out of the descriptions in the Song of Solomon? A woman made of stone walls and running water, with bunches of dates for breasts? It sounds absurd enough just to say it: to try and compose a visual picture would be preposterous. None of us needs to be convinced of that. We all know this literature is poetry. It is saying things about people and their behaviour that are undoubtedly true, but which are not literal descriptions of plain facts. There are certain areas of life where brute facts are not much help – and this is one of them. Suppose I was asked to describe my own wife and partner, and my reply was: 'She is five feet six inches tall, with brown hair and green eyes, and she drives a blue car.' My questioner would be entitled to wonder if I really knew this person well at all. Anyone could gather such facts together, merely by observation and by consulting the national records office to find out when she was born. The facts would be indisputably true – but they would not be any sort of adequate description of this person. To gain any meaningful insight into another person's character and identity, value judgments would be needed, emotive language may be used, including talk of 'love' and other more or less nebulous concepts that would be difficult to pin down, but which all of us would readily comprehend. Moreover, it would be perfectly possible to give this kind of description without once referring to the 'facts' about the individual's size, date of birth, colour of hair, and so on.

What relevance does all this have to reading and understanding the Bible? Just this: that the way we comprehend any given piece of writing or conversation depends on its style, or genre as the literary analysts would call it. The kind of literature that a book is will help to indicate what definitions of 'truth' are appropriate in any particular circumstances. Sometimes 'truth' is a matter of the reporting of literal facts – what you would have seen with your own eyes and heard with your own ears had you been there yourself. Actually, that itself is quite difficult, for another person can only report what *they* saw and heard, not what *you* would have done. Apart from that, though, what the 'truth' is will often assume a far less predictable form altogether, especially when it deals with personal relationships. Since the Bible's message is essentially about God's personal relationships with this world and its people, this kind of personally discerned 'truth' assumes a correspondingly large significance in the Bible.

The expectations we bring to Bible passages at this point can have a profound effect on what we think the Bible is saying to us. In the book of Revelation, there is a vivid description of the work of seven angels who blow seven trumpets and thereby impose various disasters upon the world and its people. As the first trumpet is blown, the writer tells us that 'Hail and fire, mixed with blood, came pouring down on the earth. A third of the earth was burnt up, a third of the trees, and every blade of green grass' (Rev 8:7). What does this say? Is it the same sort of statement as Robert Burns made when he claimed his love would endure 'till all the seas go dry... and the rocks melt in the sun'? Or is it intended to be a literal, scientific description of some terrifying (un)natural catastrophe yet to befall the world? The answer to that question makes a large difference to what we might conclude the passage will mean! Or take another example, this time from the Old Testament. Among the stories of the book of Judges is the graphic account of how Deborah, assisted by her allies, overcame a powerful Canaanite leader named Sisera. One of the causes for his downfall is said to be that 'the stars fought from the sky; as they moved across the sky, they fought against Sisera' (Judges 5:20). Is that statement meant to imply a celestial dimension to the battle – a primeval *Star Wars* – or is it the language of exaggerated poetry, vividly celebrating the extent of Deborah's victory? Most people would immediately recognise these two examples as the work of a poet, using carefully crafted and highly coloured language that was never intended to *report* literal facts, but instead was a commentary on their meaning. Other Bible passages are a bit more ambiguous, and could be understood both literally and metaphorically, depending on the intuitions of different readers. For instance, when David had been delivered from Saul, his rival, he celebrated the occasion in these words: 'The Lord reached down from above and took hold of me; God plucked me out of the deep waters' (2 Samuel 22:17). Did David get literally wet in these 'waters', then to be rescued by a physical hand reaching out of the sky? And what about Psalm 74:13,14, where God's action in creation is described in terms of smashing the multiple heads of various dragons and sea-monsters, in order to establish order for people to live?

Of course, not all sections of the Bible raise questions like these. Many more appear to be very meticulous in specifying time and place of what they describe – as when Luke begins his story of Jesus with the statement that 'it was the fifteenth year of the rule of the emperor Tiberius; Pontius Pilate was governor of Judea, Herod was ruler of Galilee, his brother Philip was ruler of the territory of Iturea and Trachonitis; Lysanius was ruler of Abilene, and Annas and Caiaphas were high priests' (Luke 3:1,2). At the very least, it looks as if he was wanting to place his story in the context of the events of real history – and even supposing that all his facts were not 100 per cent correct, he is clearly saying that the facts about Jesus' life are open to historical investigation. He is not offering only random reflections showing how a disciple felt about Jesus: he is trying to show Jesus as he actually was. In fact, the way Luke has evidently used historical procedures in constructing his twin books, Luke and Acts, only serves to reinforce that impression (Luke 1:1–4, Acts 1:1).

Perhaps I have already prolonged this point further than is necessary. But it is an important matter in relation to Bible understanding. In everyday life, we all make adjustments to different kinds of literature without consciously thinking about it. We would not demand of poetry the same kind of literal precision that we would from a textbook on surgery. To do so would destroy and invalidate it as poetry! Nor would we expect a newspaper to report things in the same kind of pedantic language as the official archives of a nation. When we go to the cinema, we do not expect that the stories presented in movies will necessarily be historically factual – though we recognise them as a 'true' presentation of the nature of human life. It is not a question of one way of looking at things being 'right' and others 'wrong'. It is simply that different sorts of presentations need to be understood in different ways, and different styles are appropriate for different purposes. Definitions of 'right' and 'wrong' here depend on the life-context. The Song of Solomon is a striking presentation of the nature of human sexuality, but that does not mean it would be possible to write either a sex manual or a handbook of gynaecology on the basis of what it contains. But if two gynaecology professors were married to each other, it is far more likely that their conversation while making love would be closer to the Song of Solomon than to the anatomical phraseology they use every day, even though that would undoubtedly be far more literally 'true' than the poetic images of the Old Testament.

Few people will have any problem with all this, because it just seems like common sense. But in Western Christianity, there has often been great resistance to applying the same common sense to our understanding of the Bible. This is the result of a legacy that goes far back into our history, through the years of the Enlightenment and back to the Reformation, if not further back still into the culture of ancient Greece. Certainly in the period following the Protestant Reformation there was a wide-ranging rejection not only of certain ideas which were seen to be contrary to scripture, but also of a whole way of looking at things. At this time, many churches and cathedrals were cleared of statues, stained-glass windows, and ornaments and relics of all kinds. The destruction of these things was symptomatic of a whole mindset that insisted on rediscovering 'the untarnished truth' about everything. There was a natural temptation to wish to find the 'plain facts' of the Bible, to accompany the equally plain and adorned church buildings in which Protestants would henceforth worship. Since anything related to the arts – dramatic as well as visual and written – was obviously neither plain nor unadorned, it was but a short step from the Reformation to the European Enlightenment, in which everything would be judged by reference to human reason, rather than feeling and intuition. From now on, the only sort of ultimate and absolute 'truth' was to be what could be proved by 'reasonable' minds, employing the techniques of 'scientific' analysis. Anything else would be dismissed as opinion, or sheer imagination – but not 'truth'. This is the way of thinking that came to be known as 'rationalism'. In theory, the church was always critical of this way of looking at things, yet paradoxically rationalism not only flourished but has penetrated deeply into many forms of modern Christianity. In the last chapter, we saw how the world of modern theology has often been dominated by the rationalist agenda. But that has not been the only place its influence was felt. Indeed, at the present time it is alive and well in many conservative forms of Christianity, where it is insisted that the 'truth' about God as revealed in the Bible must always be a matter of what can be discerned in a literal, historical, or scientific context – and where poetry, fiction, drama and the visual arts are eliminated as potential vehicles for God to communicate with either the world or its people. To proceed like that is to put human reason in the place of divine revelation. If God is truly God – all-knowing, all-understanding, ever-present – is it likely that divine 'truth' would only ever be communicated in the restricted forms of knowledge that can pass the test of narrow-minded Western rationalists? That question is being asked with increasing force by Christians from the two-thirds world today, as well as by increasing numbers of Western people who can now appreciate that, despite many benefits, the detached scientific approach to life has not actually improved things and enabled us to be better people. Increasingly, there is an emerging consensus that scientific, rational concepts of truth are but one part of the whole picture, and maybe not the most important part at that. 'Truth' comes in many different forms, and if we ignore that we shall soon tie ourselves in knots when reading the Bible. For the Bible also presents many faces, and uses many different genres to present its central message: historical narratives, poetry, letters, political manifestos – and much more besides. In chapter 3 we noted how the Bible is a collection of many books, written by many people in different contexts, and using a variety of literary styles. We have already attempted to describe these writings in relation to the cultural and social situations in which they originated. But that by itself is not enough. We also need to take note of the literary type of the various books, and even of different sections within the same book. I wonder what would happen if we took the Bible to pieces, bound all its parts as separate books (which, of course, they were to begin with), and then took them along to a librarian who had never seen them before. I would be fairly confident that they would not all be put on the same shelf. A quick look through the list of contents will soon show us why.

Let's begin with the Old Testament. Some of the longest books have every appearance of being history books of some sort. Genesis, Joshua, Judges, 1 and 2 Samuel, 1 and 2 Kings, 1 and 2 Chronicles, together with Ezra and Nehemiah, all appear to tell the story of the nation of Israel at various stages of its history. Then there are other books that are mostly, or entirely poetry. Psalms, Lamentations, Song of Solomon, Job, Ecclesiastes, and Proverbs are all written in a poetic style – though a closer look at them reveals significant differences. The first three are much like any other anthology of poetic works, though their subject matter is somewhat restricted. But the others are more like philosophical discussions, written in the style of poetry. Beyond this, most readers would find it difficult to be precise about the exact nature of much of the rest of the Old Testament. Certainly, some obviously contain laws (Exodus, Leviticus, Numbers, Deuteronomy) – but they turn out to be an unexpected mixture of civil and religious laws, together with some stories that appear to have no direct and specific connection with the legal material, but which may be history. Then there are many other writings that seem to contain social, political and religious comment on various aspects of Israelite society and culture over a long period of time. These books are identified simply by the names of the people from whom their contents originated – the prophets – and vary in length from a single page to quite extensive volumes. Here again, some parts of these writings are in poetic form, while others are narratives. Then there are other books whose precise nature is not at all certain: Ruth, Esther and Jonah. Some think of them as books of history, and would place them alongside Samuel, Kings and the rest. Others observe that the Old Testament history writers did not generally show much interest in personal biographies, and prefer to think of these books as novels. Perhaps they are not tied to one place and time, so much as probing the challenges of life in a way that is all the more relevant in all places and times precisely because of that.

Fortunately for us, we do not need to depend only on the instincts of modern librarianship in order to gain an insight into the literary character of the various Old Testament books. Long before Christians got their hands on them and called them the 'Old' Testament to distinguish them from their own 'New' Testament, they were (and still are) the Scriptures of the Jewish faith (the Hebrew Bible). They were originally organised in a rather different order, which itself tells us something of how they should be understood. The order of the books in the Christian Old Testament was taken from a Greek translation that was made during the course of the two or three centuries immediately preceding the Christian era (and known as the Septuagint, or LXX for short). But the original Hebrew Bible arranged the books in three distinct sections.

## The Law

This consisted of the books from Genesis to Deuteronomy, which are also sometimes called the 'Pentateuch'. The term 'Law', or its Hebrew equivalent 'Torah', is a more exact description of what we find in them, just so long as we remember that 'law' for the Old Testament is not quite the same thing as most of us think of when we hear that word today. Lawyers presumably view it differently, but for many people the law is a dry and dusty business, concerned with complex rules, regulations and procedures that need the expertise of those with special training to understand and apply it. Certainly, modern law is a very technical affair, and ordinary people are soon out of their depth, which is why they leave it all to the experts. But the Hebrew word *torah* is much broader than that. It does include statements of precedents and examples of specific rules, but the word itself means 'guidance' or 'instruction' – in all areas of life, not just 'legal affairs'. Consequently, the Law of the Old Testament provides guidance about God – what sort of God is to be worshipped, how God relates to the world, and what this means for people and their spirituality. Indeed, this is the whole basis for the social framework within which the Old Testament operates. The nature of God was itself the model for the ideal society. God's character could be discovered in the moral structures of the world, as well as in the distinctive episodes of Israel's history. So, for example, the Law decrees that slaves should be set free in certain circumstances, because 'you were slaves in Egypt and the Lord your God set you free' (Deuteronomy 15:15). Many other legal precepts are based on the same assumption: God's own behaviour is the pattern for human behaviour. This helps to explain why 'the Law' contains much that we might be inclined to classify as 'history'. The two were closely connected, and such 'history' as the Old Testament contains is not there merely to be a record of what happened in the past, but is preserved because of what can be learned from it for living in the present. It is not an archive repeating in a factual way what has taken place: it is a source of inspiration, highlighting incidents that are significant because of what they say about God's personality and purpose for humankind.

## The Prophets

This same theme runs through the sections of the Old Testament which Judaism grouped together as 'the prophets'. Naturally, this includes the large books of Isaiah, Jeremiah, and Ezekiel, along with the smaller writings from Hosea to Malachi. But these were called 'the latter prophets'. The 'former prophets' were actually the books that we would certainly be inclined to label as 'history' – Joshua, Judges, 1 and 2 Samuel, 1 and 2 Kings. The messages of the prophets themselves were essentially comments on the state of society at any given time. In theory, God's people ought to live in accordance with God's will. But the reality rarely matched up to the ideal – and the prophets spoke on God's behalf, announcing what things looked like when compared (and mostly contrasted) with God's standards. The Old Testament history books – 'former prophets' – are a part of this same process. They consist of an analysis of selected episodes from the past, viewed from the perspective of God's love for his people. Things are not explained here on the basis of historical cause and effect, but by reference to God's law. Obedience to God was high at those times when Israel prospered; disobedience, however, often went hand-in-hand with national decline. This is obviously 'history with a bias', if you like. The authors knew they were loved by God, and wanted their people to share that experience. This approach to history writing certainly leaves a number of loose ends untied for today's readers who come to the Old Testament searching for a comprehensive 'history of Israel', for these books were never intended to be a mere collection of chronicles about the past. That does not in itself invalidate or place a question mark against the 'truth' of Old Testament history writing. I referred earlier in this chapter to two possible ways I might describe my wife: by stating 'the facts', or by sharing my personal reflections on her character. I suggested that the first by itself would give rather an inadequate picture. In ordinary, secular history we expect a historian to tell us not only what the facts are, but what it all means, and historians write from a variety of perspectives, depending on how they see life and its meaning. The people whose insights inspired the Old Testament historians were the great prophets, who were convinced that life only makes sense when God is included in it.

## The writings

Finally, the Hebrew Bible contains the Writings. This is, in effect, what is left when the Law and Prophets are removed, for there is no particular cohesion in this group of documents: Psalms, Proverbs, Job, Ruth, Song of Solomon, Ecclesiastes, Lamentations, Esther, Daniel, Ezra, Nehemiah, 1 and 2 Chronicles. They were probably grouped together because they were compiled last of all, and include various types of literature. Psalms is all poetry – hymns, used in the praise of God in the Jerusalem Temple, after the return from exile in Babylon, but containing songs first written many centuries before. Proverbs and Song of Solomon deal with such universal topics (parental advice to children, and sexual love) that they are almost timeless, and could have been first written down almost anywhere. Ecclesiastes and Lamentations ask ultimate questions about the meaning of life and the nature of morality – while Ezra, Nehemiah, and Chronicles are a fresh appraisal of the meaning of Judah's history, this time in light of the fact that the exile did not lead to final extinction for the nation. Ruth, Esther and the first section of Daniel tell of the Jewish heroes whose names they bear, and draw lessons from their experiences, while the second part of Daniel contains a complex series of visions trying to make sense out of the fact that evil people seem to prosper and the good suffer. The book of Job explores the same theme, though from a different angle altogether. Some of these books are not difficult to classify, while others arouse strong debate and controversy. Is there an element of fiction writing in some of them, and is Job, with its extended dialogues between its hero, his friends and God intended to be the script for an acted drama? Perhaps we shall never know the answer to some of these questions – though whatever our answer, we can still expect to discover something of God in them. But these books are the exceptions, for on the whole it is not at all difficult to see the various types of literature that have gone together to make up the Old Testament.

When we come to the New Testament, we find a selection of different sorts of literature. Whereas the Old Testament was the national archive of a state, the New Testament contains a more arbitrary collection of writings, relating to the life of a minority group within the all-powerful Roman empire in the first century AD. At the time, Christianity was not a permitted religion under Roman law, though it was generally tolerated. But life was hard and difficult for most Christians: many of them were slaves, and their opportunities for literary and artistic pursuits must have been limited. According to one source, even some of the leading figures in the early church were 'ignorant and uneducated' (Acts 4:13). That probably does not mean they were totally illiterate, but it certainly indicates that Peter and John had not received the formal education that was typical of the Greek and Roman poets of their day.

The range of literature found in the New Testament is much more restricted than the contents of the Old. There is nothing comparable with the magnificent poetry of the book of Psalms, for instance – either in scope or sheer size. But that does not necessarily mean the early Christians were not poets and song-writers, for several snippets of early Christian verse are in fact quoted and referred to in other New Testament contexts (eg Philippians 2:6–11; 1 Timothy 3:16; 2 Timothy 2:11–13).

The first parts of the New Testament to be written down were the letters that Paul and other apostolic leaders sent to their friends in various parts of the Roman empire. As Christian communities spread through the successful evangel-istic work of the followers of Jesus, it was important to keep in touch with them. The practice of Paul, and perhaps of others too, was to appoint local leaders in the new churches, and then move on to preach in other areas themselves. This had the advantage of encouraging the converts to grow spiritually and to develop their own indigenous styles of ministry, rather than having a pattern imposed from outside. But it also meant most congregations lacked men and women of longer experience and greater knowledge, who could advise and guide from the perspective of a broader understanding. For that, they needed to be in touch with their founding apostles, and writing letters was the fastest way to do this. Letters were commonly sent by hand with a personal messenger, and he or she would usually carry part of the message to be delivered orally. We can see this process at work in many of Paul's letters, which were sent in reply either to written notes or verbal messages from his con-verts. 1 and 2 Corinthians, Galatians, Philippians, Colossians, 1 and 2 Thessalonians, Philemon – and perhaps others – were all penned because of specific news that had come to Paul in this way. Paul was not the only letter writer among the early churches. The names of Peter and John, as well as James and Jude (two lesser known leaders, probably in more local circum-stances) are all attached to various New Testament letters.

But there are other types of literature in the New Testament besides letters, notably the Gospels (Matthew, Mark, Luke and John), and the book of Acts, which cannot be separated from the Gospel of Luke, for the two of them are separate volumes of what is essentially the same work. Like the letters, these books were also written to support the evangelistic and pastoral work of the churches. To the modern reader looking at the Gospels for the first time, they perhaps look like biographies of Jesus. They certainly contain a good deal of information about his teachings and his style of life, but they are not biography in the normal sense of the word. For one thing, apart from Luke they tell us nothing at all about either his childhood or youth. Two of them – Mark and John – do not even mention Jesus' birth. Yet they all describe in considerable detail Jesus' death and resurrection, and the events of the weeks preceding that – together with a selection of other incidents taken from a period of only about three years of his adult life. The reason for this unusual balance of material about Jesus is made quite explicit by the writer of John's Gospel. There it is explained that the information preserved in the Gospel is just a small section from a much larger body of knowledge (John 20:30, 21:25), and that the selection has been made in accordance with the evangelistic purpose of the writer: 'these have been written *in order that you may believe* that Jesus is the Messiah, the Son of God, and that through your faith in him you may have life' (John 20:31). John was not writing primarily out of historical curiosity. He was, rather, using historical materials and applying them in such a way that they would address the needs and questions of people in the world of his own day (probably towards the end of the first century).

Matthew preserves a very different selection of materials about Jesus' life and teaching – this time arranged not so much for the benefit of those outside the church, but for the concerns of those newly converted. Indeed, Matthew has organised the story of Jesus in a topical way, to give new converts ready access to the key elements of Jesus' teaching as it might apply to them. It is Matthew who gathers together the 'Sermon on the Mount' as a compilation of the most striking things Jesus said about how disciples should behave. This is also the Gospel which gives us the Lord's Prayer in a form that would be particularly appropriate for regular repetition in worship (Matthew 6:9–13). Mark has also made a selective presentation of the life of Jesus. He also majors on the question of discipleship, though in a more robust way than Matthew. How should disciples deal with persecution? Is suffering an unavoidable part of the Christian life? What should Christians believe about Jesus himself? These questions, and others, were no doubt being asked by Christians whom Mark knew – probably in Rome about the middle of the first century – and he uses the stories about Jesus to answer them. Then we come to Luke, whose work is one of the most accomplished pieces of writing in the whole New Testament, and has much in common with the polished books of classical Greek and Latin authors. Like John, he is quite open about explaining his strategy: he has read what others had written about Jesus (probably including Mark), and set out to make his own account on that basis (Luke 1:1–4). This is the way that a self-conscious historian would work – sifting sources, checking facts, and putting them all together in a new and creative way. Luke's story in Acts is also selective, and concerns mostly the exploits of Paul. Apart from a few accounts of their activity in the earliest days of the church in Jerusalem, other important leaders like John and Peter are scarcely mentioned, and even Paul's life is not covered in every detail. To write a biography of Paul, we need to amalgamate the evidence of Paul's own letters with the narrative of Acts. Luke was a companion of Paul during much of his missionary work. He was probably not a Jew himself, and his selection of materials reflects that. In Acts, his main emphasis is on showing how the structures of the Roman empire were able to facilitate the spread of the church – and in the process to commend the Christian faith to educated Romans like Theophilus to whom his two books are addressed. As part of this message, Luke records Paul's many dealings with Roman officials, and tells how he ultimately reached Rome. In his Gospel, Luke also deals with other issues that Gentiles would be likely to raise. How did Jesus himself relate to non-Jews? And to women, and other minority groups? And was the explanation for the dynamic spread of the church to be found in the ministry of Jesus himself? Luke answered that by drawing attention to the way the Holy Spirit was at work both in Jesus' ministry and in the work of his disciples after him. The New Testament Gospels are, in their own way, not so different from the history books of the Old Testament. They were not written by detached observers who simply reported the facts, but by Christians who were seeking to commend their faith by using the facts to share with others the difference that belief in Jesus had made in their own lives.

Finally, the New Testament contains two other books which fit into none of the categories discussed so far: Hebrews and Revelation. Both are one-off productions. Revelation is much like the Old Testament book of Daniel, and contains a similar series of visions exploring the ultimate meaning and destiny of the world and its people. Hebrews is a semi-philosophical discussion of the nature of belief in Jesus when it is related to its origins in Judaism and the Old Testament. It too is full of symbolism, though of a different sort to Revelation. It includes much allegory and typology, in which historical events and people are treated as illustrations of deeper meanings in life. This way of thinking had first been popularised by the Jewish writer Philo of Alexandria, and it was to have considerable influence on the way the Bible was understood in the next three or four centuries.

Facts like these are the basic raw materials out of which modern study of the Bible has been fashioned. At one time, reading and understanding the Bible was a bit like pulling rabbits out of hats. As long as words could be found that appeared to be vaguely relevant to a contemporary situation, then the original meaning or context of a passage was not strictly relevant. But we can now see that things are not so simple. The same words can vary in meaning depending on the context in which they are used. And when we can identify many different types of literature in the Bible, then the possibilities for understanding and misunderstanding are vast and expansive.

Is it then a hopeless task for the average Christian to be able to penetrate both the history and cultural forms of the Bible, and to discover its essential message for today's world? It must be admitted that – at least for many Western people – the Bible would be a good deal easier to handle if it had come down to us in the form of propositional statements about theology rather than as a mixed collection of different books from varied historical and social settings. At least if it consisted of abstract truths about God, we would be able to pin it down with far less trouble. But the God of whom the Bible speaks does not come into our lives like that. 'God' is not a book of theology, or an abstract symbol of eternal things, but a person who meets with us in the trivial and ordinary affairs of every day, as well as in unique and unrepeatable acts like the exodus or the birth of Jesus. In chapter 4 it was suggested that the faith of the early church could be roughly summed up in the statement of John 1:14, 'The Word became a human being and, full of grace and truth, lived among us'. But that message is not restricted only to one book of the Bible: it runs like a golden thread through the fabric of them all. For God to be a person means that spiritual encounters can take place at all points of human experience: at times of celebration just as easily as in moments of deep crisis. God is there in the hour of suffering and death, as well as sharing in the joys of love-making and birth. God is not limited by the boundaries of time and space, but relates to the whole of life – laws and institutions, as well as past history, future hopes, and personal ambitions. As one of the Old Testament prophets put it, 'I am a God who is everywhere and not in one place only. No one can hide where I cannot see them. Do you not know that I am everywhere in heaven and on earth?' (Jeremiah 23:23,24).

One of the most distinctive aspects of the Christian faith is the insistence that God is not locked up in the remote confines of holy places, nor in the equally inscrutable recesses of abstruse theological dogma. Just as God became a human person in Jesus, with all the risk of misunderstanding that entailed, so God's word comes to us in many different shapes and forms, addressing us in the many and varied circumstances of life. This is the starting point from which we can begin to unpack what it can mean for ordinary people to understand the Bible for themselves today – and that is where we now head in the next chapter.

*Chapter 6*

# Learning to use a compass

In some previous chapters there has been a good deal of emphasis on the distinctiveness of the Bible, as we have looked at the differences between the world of the Bible and the world in which we live today. At some points, the differences have even been exaggerated a little, and I would not apologise for doing so, for this is an important part of getting the Bible in a true perspective. We need to remember that every part of the Bible comes to us today as a message from an alien culture, which none of us has ever known for ourselves. Regardless of what we may have in common with them, we are not actually the same as ancient Canaanites or Egyptians, Romans or Greeks, and in most respects the way such people thought and wrote needs to be interpreted and reformulated before it can have any impact on us today. But we must not allow that consideration to blind us to the fact that there are many close similarities between the Bible and our experience as Christians today – and these similarities are just as important as the differences.

Being a Christian is very closely related to being a part of the community of the church. Sometimes we need to stress that knowing God is a personal affair, distinct and special for each of us – and so it is. But we can never serve and worship God in isolation from others. We know God most thoroughly in shared experiences with other Christians. That is how God intended it to be, for the gospel is not an inward-looking pietistic mysticism, but a life-changing message that relates directly to the continuing life of a community. The Old Testament lays great emphasis on the importance of Israel being a nation where God was worshipped and served, and even down to the smallest details, the way life was organised ought to reflect the loving character of God. As Christians, we may find difficulties with stories like that of the unfortunate Achan, who was done to death because of his disobedience over an apparently trivial affair (Joshua 7). But it is not difficult to see the point of the incident within its own context: the people of God were to keep themselves pure, so they could worthily serve a God whose own most important characteristic was 'holiness'. The same notion of a community which belongs to God and reflects the values and standards of the gospel is central to the New Testament too. Indeed, in many respects the church seems to be conceived of as the continuation and fulfilment of what Old Testament Israel had been. Certainly Paul calls (Gentile) Christians 'the Israel of God' (Galatians 6:16), and in 1 Peter a number of important Old Testament statements about Israel are applied to Christian believers (1 Peter 2:1–10). We also find the same concern that the church should be a community set apart for God (Romans 12:1) – though this was typically achieved by rather less drastic measures than those used in some Old Testament stories.

All this has a significant bearing on our understanding of the Bible today. It means that the Bible books had their origins in the life of communities worshipping God – and Christians today are a part of that same community every bit as much as was Abraham, or Amos, Peter, or Paul. A hundred years ago, experts on the Bible spent a good deal of energy trying to find out with precision just where all the Bible books came from. Who wrote them, and when and why? Did Moses really write the Pentateuch, David the Psalms, or Matthew the Gospel that now bears his name? The search for ultimate origins had of course been one of the obsessions of nineteenth century thinkers in many fields of enquiry. Charles Darwin spent much of his life trying to find out where the world came from, in the hope that by so doing he could discover the ultimate meaning of it all. Bible scholars applied themselves with the same rigorous discipline to find out where the Bible came from. They too hoped by this means to fathom out what it all means. But if you ask where a thing comes from, then the best you can hope for is to find out where it came from! It might well be useful and illuminating to know that, but it does not by itself answer the rather different question, 'What does it all mean?'

Much ink was used up, and many erudite volumes written in the search for the Bible's origins. Some ideas have stood the test of time, but many more are now seen to be simply absurd. In any event, more recent research has suggested that these questions are not after all as important as some people once imagined. The Old Testament book of Psalms can illustrate this. It is possible to dissect every one of its 150 psalms and ask who wrote them – but if we think only of this question, we are likely to miss their lasting relevance. In fact, when we realise that they were gathered together as the hymn book of the Temple built in the days of Haggai and Zechariah, after the exile in Babylon, we have an immediate relationship with them – regardless of who actually penned them in the first place. For these wonderful poems are included in the Bible as a mirror of the beliefs, aspirations, and emotions of the people of God – and today's Christians are a part of the same people of God. A closer look shows that the psalms are not all that different from any modern hymn book. There are songs of praise (eg 8, 29, 33); songs of thanks expressing gratitude to God for past blessings (30, 32, 34); and there are prayers for deliverance from hostile powers (44, 74, 79) and for help in personal circumstances (3, 5, 7, 13). It is typical of the over-rationalised approach of the Enlightenment for people to feel a great urge to allocate the psalms to this or that event in the life of David or the history of Israel, instead of accepting the emotional appeal of their sentiments, and thereby entering into the atmosphere of worship and humble fellowship with God that they were originally designed to engender. We will certainly get to know God better by entering into the atmosphere of devotion that pervades its pages than by taking the Bible apart as if it was a lifeless corpse.

The same approach can also enhance our appreciation of other parts of Scripture. The New Testament Gospels are a further example where we can find many illuminating insights by asking how they were relevant to the life of the earliest church, rather than by merely trying to discover the identities of Matthew, Mark, Luke and John. For each of these writers was addressing the church and society in which they happened to be living. In some senses therefore what they wrote presents a mosaic image of the life of the earliest Christian communities. They reflect their problems and questions, as well as their joys and triumphs. That is not to say that they do not also give us accounts of certain aspects of Jesus' life and teaching. Of course they do, and to suggest otherwise would run in the face of all the evidence. But we only have access to Jesus at these particular points because the Gospel writers felt the incidents and statements they related had a further relevance to the ongoing life of their own churches. When we read the Gospels with this in mind, we can see them in a new light, for even familiar teaching is often put to different uses in the various Gospels. What is the point of the parable of the lost sheep? You might think the answer is straightforward, but when we actually go to the Gospels, we discover two quite distinct answers to that question. In Luke, the lost sheep is a sinner who is found and brought into fellowship with God (15:1-7), whereas in Matthew, the lost sheep is 'one of these little ones' who are already part of God's kingdom, but who has strayed away from the true fold (18:12-14). We need not doubt that Jesus himself told such a parable, but the creative use to which each author has put the parable gives us an added insight not only into the mind of Jesus, but also into ways in which his teaching can be applied to the needs of different circumstances. The same thing is true at other places too. Why else would there be two different versions of the Lord's Prayer (Matthew 6:9-13, Luke 11:2-4) – or, in the Old Testament, two forms of the Ten Commandments (Exodus 20:1-17, Deuteronomy 5:6-21)? Obviously, in different situations the same basic teaching could be applied to answer the diverse questions of those to whom it was addressed. There are many hundreds of such examples throughout the Bible. We noticed in chapter 4 how Hosea presents a different angle on Jehu from that contained in the book of Kings – because the questions and needs of his generation were different from the concerns that were most pressing when the Old Testament history books were written. But we also find Daniel taking up some aspects of Jeremiah's messages, and giving them a new significance in the light of changing circumstances (Daniel 9:1–2) – and in Isaiah 43 the exodus from Egypt is given a new importance as a model of what will happen to the exiles in Babylon many generations later. The most striking example of all is the way in which Old Testament references to the kings in Jerusalem were later understood as prophecies about the coming of a Messiah to save God's people (eg Psalm 2:7–8, Isaiah 7:10–16, and many others). It is hardly surprising that over the thousand years or so that the Old Testament was being written, such up-dating and reapplying of its message should have taken place. But even in the far shorter time-span represented by the New Testament books, we can see some indications of the same process – not only within the Gospels, but also with Paul's letters, which 2 Peter 3:16 tells us required careful analysis and application to be made relevant to other situations than those they originally addressed.

We must be careful not to exaggerate this, but there is a clear sense in which the Bible is a continual process of bringing God's word to bear on many different situations at different times and places. This fact gives us a further insight into what is involved in understanding the Bible's message for ourselves today. When I was a student, I remember being told that the science of Bible interpretation ('hermeneutics') was now so refined and 'scientific' that by the methodical application of certain principles it would be possible to arrive at a totally unbiased and 'objective' view of what the Bible has to say. The term 'presuppositionless exegesis' was much talked about as a means of describing this process. Put simply, it was assumed that you could put a Bible before a Jew, a Muslim, a Christian and an atheist, and, if they all kept to the rules, emptied their minds of in-built prejudice and presuppositions, then they would all reach exactly the same conclusions. I was rather sceptical about it then, and more recent experience has not changed my mind. No doubt it is the case that, in terms of actually translating the Bible from its original languages, the four assorted characters mentioned could – in principle anyway – come up with the same rendering. The same potential also perhaps exists if we are talking about an understanding of some of the history contained in the Bible – though here the challenge would undoubtedly be far greater. But if the Bible is really about God's relationships with the world and its people, rather than just about language, or history, or 'science', what value would there be in a totally detached, 'objective' and 'scientific' description of that anyway? I have already suggested that in describing my wife, for instance, there would be little point in restricting such a description to the 'facts'. Any worthwhile comment on her would need to reflect the personal dimension of such a relationship, and what is true of human relationships must surely be true of our knowledge of God. In any case, it is an exceedingly hard thing to rid ourselves of presuppositions, and quite impossible to evacuate the mind in such a total way that the Bible can be read 'objectively' as if we had never seen it before. The fact is that we all have our preconceptions about the Bible, whether positive or negative. It is possible to take account of these, and we should do so whenever we can, by asking if we are reaching this or that conclusion because we have always thought that anyway – or because it is genuinely coming to us out of study of the text. If we find things we would have thought in any case apparently coming from the text, then we need to pause and ask more searching questions at those points. To that extent, it is possible at least to try and be 'presuppositionless'.

But is it either necessary or desirable to adopt a neutral stance in reading the Bible, or any other piece of literature, for that matter? Will the Bible not be more relevant to our lives if we come to it as we are, complete with all our hang-ups, inhibitions and preconceptions? Is there not an important sense in which we bring something to the text, addressing it with the questions that we want to ask, as well as listening to what it has to say to us from a dim and distant historical past? After all, this is the way we would expect to read any other great work of literature. By all means ask William Shakespeare where he found the plots for his plays, or quiz D H Lawrence about the real-life situations at the back of his works – but in the final analysis, most readers of their books look not just for such literary and historical facts, but for some insights that will speak out of their past directly into the concerns of the present. If we have that expectation of secular writers, how much more ought Christians to expect that the word of God should come to us with a living impact, making itself relevant to our concerns in the present day? In point of fact, many parts of the Bible actually demand a personal interaction on the part of the reader. We have already mentioned the Psalms, with their open invitation to share in the worship of the God whose love and power they celebrate. But what about the parables of Jesus? Does it make sense to read them as a 'detached observer'? It is certainly possible to do so, and to look at a story such as the Good Samaritan as an illustration of social tensions between Jews and their Samaritan neighbours in the first century AD. But to do so misses the point of it all, which is summed up in the final phrase: 'You go and do the same' (Luke 10:37). What is true here is also the case with most of Jesus' teaching, for he speaks in such a way that it is clear he is not only announcing the arrival of God's kingdom in a theoretical way – he is inviting others to join in. Five hundred years ago, Christians all over Europe had no doubt that the Bible demanded this kind of personal interaction by those who read or (in their case) heard its words. The art galleries of the world are full of works by medieval artists, based on the life and times of Jesus. The crucifixion was a favourite theme, and there are many works showing Jesus hanging on a cross between the two thieves. But when we look more closely, it is clear that this is no 'objective' presentation of what a bystander would have actually witnessed. The people standing around the crosses regularly look strangely out of place. Instead of Roman soldiers and Palestinian peasants, we see soldiers and peasants of the sixteenth century, while the skyline of the city where the crucifixion takes place is also historically anachronistic – even inaccurate – for the scene takes place not in Jerusalem in AD 33, but in Venice or Rome in 1500. Historical purists will argue that everything is wrong here. The crucifixion cannot possibly have been like that. But most of us would not feel that way. Looking at the occasion from the perspective of a different age, and with changed expectations, in no way invalidates the reality of what the cross is. Indeed, we may instinctively follow the artists' example, and sketch in an image of ourselves and our own society – thereby moving the scene onto a more profound level altogether.

People trained in modern Western education sometimes find it hard to do this. We have been taught not to trust our feelings. They are subjective and unreliable, we are told – certainly not rational or scientific. As a result, some find it a real struggle to accept their emotions as an authentic part of human existence – to our great impoverishment! But when we allow ourselves to bring to our Bible reading all the everyday questions and problems that perplex us, we can gain a totally fresh understanding of what God can say to us through its pages. Some of the most striking examples of how the Bible can come alive in today's world are found not in Western cultures, but among the growing churches of the two-thirds world. The Bible has been one of the key elements in the great expansion of world Christianity that has occurred during the last fifty years or so. All over the world, small groups of people have come together to read and study it for the first time, and discovered that it speaks directly to their own situation. For many of these people, life is a constant struggle against injustice, oppression and exploitation of various sorts – so does the Bible have anything relevant to say about issues like that? The question itself is not new. It was being asked 150 years ago by Africans who had been enslaved in the southern states of America. But because they were largely illiterate, they had no way of looking for the answer themselves. Instead they had to depend on their white (and mostly Christian) owners, who told them that though things may be bad in this life, there was hope for a better future in heaven, even for slaves. That was a traditional Western answer of the time, based on the belief that, if the Bible is about God, it must be about religion, and religion deals with things related to the life of some other world, not this one. There is of course an element of truth in all that, and we should never lose sight of the transcendental, other-worldly strand in the Bible's message. But Christians in other parts of the world have been reminding us that God's word is as relevant for life in this world as it is for the life of the next.

When the Bible is read in this way, its message unexpectedly comes to life in new ways. For example, Christians have read the Old Testament story of the exodus for generations, and have generally sought to understand it in one of two ways. Firstly, as a historical event: the story has been carefully examined from every conceivable angle, to try to articulate exactly what it was that happened, and how it fits into other parts of Canaanite and Israelite history. We need scarcely doubt that there was a historical exodus, but knowing that only enlightens us about an episode in ancient history. It does not of itself tell us much about God. That is why interpreters have often asked a further question: is there some hidden, symbolic meaning in all this, that directly comments on some aspects of Christian belief and theology? By reading the exodus story not as history, but as an allegorical and symbolic presentation of Christian truth, it was not too difficult to find such meanings. A common view was that the exodus was a symbol of the truths that come to full expression in Christian salvation and baptism. Escape from Egypt, under the protection of the blood of the Passover lamb, and through the waters of the Red Sea, was comparable to escape from sin through the agency of Christ's death and Christian baptism. The parallel was never exact, of course, for the whole point of the exodus story was that no one got wet, whereas baptism always implied that they did. But the similarities were nevertheless near enough for the 'true meaning' of the exodus to be discovered in this way. When looked at from the point of view of the poor and dispossessed in today's world, however, the same story takes on a different appearance. What was actually going on here? The answer seems obvious: a group of people under the domination of a totalitarian dictatorship, with no hope of any personal or national fulfilment, were delivered into a land of their own, where they could live as free men and women. How did all this come about? By the powerful acts of God, who both conceived and orchestrated the great escape. What, then, does this say about the God of the Bible? At the very least, that

God is on the side of the poor rather than the powerful – and that God's will can be demonstrated and carried through by direct intervention in the affairs of this world, as slaves are set free and society is given a new direction.

The exodus story is not the only one that takes on new meaning when read from within the life context of today's world. The life and teaching of Jesus also yields new insights – or, at least, insights that Christians have generally chosen to ignore over the centuries. When disinherited people begin to read the story of the first Christmas, among the first statements they come to are in the Magnificat. Mary's song of praise, even before Jesus was born, celebrates the fact that with his birth 'God has brought down mighty kings from their thrones, and lifted up the lowly... filled the hungry with good things, and sent the rich away with empty hands' (Luke 1:52,53). A few pages further on, in his sermon in the synagogue at Nazareth, Jesus declares (quoting the Old Testament), 'The Spirit of the Lord is upon me, because God has chosen me to bring good news to the poor... to proclaim liberty to the captives and recovery of sight to the blind; to set free the oppressed...' (Luke 4:18,19). These passages have always been there, but the customary mindset of Christianity tended to 'spiritualise' them, and it has taken the new insights of those who are actually disadvantaged and suffering in today's world to help us see that the message of the Bible does have something important to say, with repercussions far beyond churches and religious services. God actually reaches down to where people are suffering, and acts decisively in their lives. As we go further into the Gospels, the parables underline the same message. Why do you suppose all the outcasts of society are goodies in the parables, while the baddies turn out to be the conventionally religious and upright?

What then does human community look like in God's kingdom? The answer to that is not far away either – in Paul's pictures of the church as the body of Christ. For the apostle, the church was to be the kingdom in miniature – a little piece of heaven on earth here and now, a living witness to God's will for humankind. For many centuries it was taken for granted that when Paul wrote of 'the church' he had in mind the sort of institutions that historically have carried that title. The Reformers saw through that, and argued for a wider notion of fellowship in the church with their ideas of 'the priesthood of all believers'. But their successors continued to set up structures that made it impossible for that ideal ever to come to any kind of practical expression. Today, people all over the world are searching for a form of community in which they can grow to full status as human beings. What is it like? Where can it be found? What form of existence will bring true fulfilment and meaning into our corporate lives? When these questions are addressed to the Bible, many are finding them answered in a way of relating that can be described as 'the body of Christ' (1 Corinthians 12). In this social context, all are equal because God has made them that way. Though there is structure, all are potentially 'office-bearers', because God's Spirit lives in each one. Moreover, here distinctions of race, social class and sex are no longer appropriate, because Christ has abolished them all (Galatians 3:28). Gustavo Gutiérrez, an eminent South American church leader, has described it in these terms:

> As read from the point of view of the poor, the gospel summons into being a people's church. A church which springs up from the people, from a people which wrenches the gospel from the hands of this world's powerful, from a people who will not allow the gospel to be used to justify a status quo that is contrary to the will of the God who liberates... We are called to build the church from below, from the poor, from the situation of the exploited classes, and the excluded races, and the despised cultures.

I am not suggesting that these new lessons emerging from the churches of the developing world are necessarily the same lessons as we need to learn in Western Christianity today. To do so would be to adopt the same blinkered mentality as our forebears did when they insisted the only possible way of articulating Christian truth was by use of the categories of European analytical philosophy. But it cannot be denied that reading the Bible and understanding it in a life-changing way, is a two-way process. An old definition of a (bad) lecture describes it as 'a process whereby the contents of the professor's notes are transferred to the student's notes without passing through the minds of either'. Many of the ways in which Christians try to communicate their faith are just like that, with no power to engage the thinking and change the lives of those who must endure them. But that is not how God comes to us. God became a person of the world, in order to offer the opportunity of a living, personal communication that can change our thinking and challenge our priorities. God offers to us the possibility of a personal relationship, which by definition means that we need to be willing to engage in meaningful dialogue. We need therefore to be honest as we approach the Bible, not hesitating to address our difficult questions to it, beginning from where we are and speaking to God from that perspective. It is in the context of such openness to God's will and God's word that the Bible can begin to come alive, as God speaks to us in ways that will effectively enhance our daily living and empower our spirituality.

## Chapter 7

# Beginning your own journey

In previous chapters we have examined many of the factors that need to be taken into account if we are to begin to understand the Bible's message for us today. We have seen the importance of reading it in ways that will be conducive to understanding, and of using a translation that is appropriate for the immediate purpose in hand. Then we looked briefly at the Bible's original life context, its social and cultural background in the ancient world, its literary forms, and its assumptions about God and the world. But still at the end of it all is this question: what can you actually do when you sit down with the Bible open in front of you? For no matter how interesting you have found this book – nor how many others like it you have on your shelves – if you are unable to get to grips with the Bible for yourself, nothing much has been achieved. Books about the Bible can be of great help in understanding it, and we should use them to the full. Yet there is a danger that Christians can spend too much time reading books about the Bible, and not take enough time to read the book itself. God never intended that the Bible should be a book only for experts. So we must now try and apply some of the lessons of previous chapters to what happens when you actually sit down with the Bible itself.

First of all, we need to remember in all talk of Bible understanding that it is ultimately the work of the Holy Spirit to make the words come alive to us. Jesus promises his disciples that 'the Holy Spirit ... will teach you everything and make you remember all that I have told you' (John 14:26). No amount of fancy interpretative techniques – however valuable in themselves – can illuminate our understanding unless we are consciously prepared to listen to what the Spirit is saying to us. This is especially important if, as the last chapter suggested, understanding the Bible is a two-way process of communication. We shall return to that principle shortly, but here let us simply note that our expectations of God are bound to affect our Bible study.

If we come to the Bible expecting to find only drab and uninteresting doctrines and theologies – then that is what we will find. But if we know and love a God who is at work in our world, doing through people today the same works as were accomplished through Jesus and the apostles, then we will be open to the possibility of Bible study becoming a real meeting-point between ourselves and the living God. The great missionary pioneer William Carey once recommended, in a different connection, that Christians should 'expect great things from God'. That is just as applicable to Bible study as it is to mission and evangelism. For generations, some Christians have thought of Bible study as a bookish kind of thing, in which what we learn must always be facts and figures about our faith. Even today it is not at all unusual to meet people, especially in student circles, who can spend hours – even days – splitting hairs about their belief in things like predestination, while all around them people have the far simpler need just to know God in a way that can challenge and change their lives. The rise of the New Age has exposed the weakness of this kind of purely intellectual faith, and has helped to identify a major reason why so many people who are searching for spiritual answers to life's questions automatically assume that the church has nothing worthwhile to say. An exclusively cerebral form of Christianity will never satisfy the human heart. Some sections of the church have consciously moved away from that, of course, most notably in the charismatic movement. Here people prefer to discern God's will not so much through Bible study as by more direct means such as visions, prophecies, pictures, words of knowledge, and so on. It is a false antithesis between thinking and feeling to imagine that we are forced to choose between these two, for the gospel is presented by Jesus as a holistic approach to life which encompasses all parts of our being – and that includes our intellectual thought processes, as well as our emotions, spirits, and bodies (Mark 12:29,30). Because of the recent history of Christianity, however, probably the less intellectual approach is the one that needs to be emphasised right now, just because most Christians take for granted that the Bible needs some serious thinking.

For God to address us through the Bible, our use of it should always be set firmly in the context of prayer and spiritual devotion. We saw in the last chapter that much of the Bible actually had its origins in the context of worship. Its books are not just collections of intellectual ideas about God: they reflect the experiences of ordinary people whose lives gained new meaning as they opened themselves up to the work of God's Spirit. It should therefore come as no surprise to learn that the Bible can usually speak to us most powerfully when we ourselves are prepared to be open to God as we read it. In a book about the Bible, I must not digress too far here to discuss the nature of prayer and worship. Let me simply say that Bible, prayer and worship together are absolute crucial elements in the ongoing process of discovering God which is at the centre of every Christian's life.

To discover God most truly also involves a fresh awareness of ourselves. For authentic worship is a process of allowing all that we know of God to address all that we know of ourselves. So when we sit down to read the Bible, the Bible itself may not be the first thing to engage our attentions. We may, for example, first spend time in reflective prayer, or worship, or meditation. Then, having become aware of our own feelings and needs, and those of others who may be with us – not to mention the wider world – we are ready to hear what God has to say to us through the Bible. One of the major weaknesses in the way we tend to use the Bible in church services is that we rarely have the opportunity to set it in such a context of open sharing and worship. As a result, Bible reading and exposition often appears as something the minister – the 'expert' – does for or to the rest of the congregation. Those of us who are ministers need to think through the implications of this carefully, so that the Bible's power to address our emotions is not restricted by our own handling of it. We also need to remember, though, that all this talk of Bible reading taking place in the context of worship does not mean we need to take a great deal of time whenever we turn to its pages. Martin Luther once remarked that 'work is worship', reminding us that every aspect of our lives as Christians should be worship of God. I ought to be as open to God while walking down the street as I am in the sanctuary of some great church building. That means, as we shall see, that the Bible can speak to me as I go about my daily business, as well as at those points in life when I am able to set aside special times for its study.

Openness to the Holy Spirit, then, is the first and most crucial element of intelligent Bible study. But notice I wrote 'intelligent' Bible study. We all have the capacity to think, and that too is one of God's gifts to us. There are no spiritual bonus points for using our brains and our commonsense in everyday work, and then shutting them in the closet when we open the Bible. Yet so many of us do exactly that – as if understanding the Bible calls for a different kind of logic from everyday life. Henry Ford once said, 'Thinking is the hardest work there is, which is probably the reason why so few people engage in it.' So be warned! Perhaps we should start by asking, why do I want to read my Bible just now? What do I want to get out of it? What am I looking for? In everyday situations, we do this all the time. The business – or church – with no aims, no objectives, and no immediate goals gets nowhere. I remember once planning to have a family day out, something that at the time was quite an achievement as it required several people's diaries to be kept free for the same day. But we all made the effort, and when the day came we were all looking forward to spending quality time with one another. There was just one problem: we couldn't decide where to go. Would it be the countryside, or the seaside, an organised day at a theme park, or in some remote spot with only the hills and the wildlife for company? No one could decide – not even when we got into the car. But we drove off all the same. As the driver, I was determined not to be 'directive', and so at the first cross-roads (not half a mile from our home) I asked the others, 'Now which way?' Following my misguided example, no one else wanted to be thought 'directive' either. The same performance was repeated at many junctions and traffic lights, with the car getting more and more steamed up in every sense of that word!

I don't suppose other parents are stupid enough to get into situations like that. But it taught me a very important lesson, not just about being a husband and father but also about life in general. We had a lot going for us on that occasion. Our motivation was impeccable, and our commitment to each other was beyond question as well, for we had all given up something in order to be there. In addition, we were prepared to put resources into it, in terms of both money and energy. When the day came, it was so packed with activity that we were all exhausted at the end of it. As we drove about, we covered an amazing mileage for just a single day's motoring. We spent a lot of time and money keeping ourselves busy, but in the process we achieved nothing satisfying at all. We actually generated a lot of animosity which we later regretted. The whole episode has gone down in our family's history as something definitely not to be repeated. Now why was this? In the last analysis, the answer is quite simple. We were all frustrated because we had no specific goals. We had a general aim, to have a pleasant day out together – but no precise idea of why or how that could be accomplished.

Life in many churches today is just like that: a lot of activity with very little achievement. So is much personal Bible reading, which is why it is worth identifying a goal at the outset. For the nature of your goal will determine the way you go about reading and thinking about your Bible. For instance, if you find yourself at 7.15 in the morning with fifteen minutes before you have to catch a bus to work, and you want to get some positive Bible reading in that time, then there is little point in turning to a long and complex passage that demands much thought. What you need at that point in life will probably be best provided by following one of the many excellent Bible reading plans, that will help you to identify a short passage, will give you a few concise observations on it, and leave you with a couple of key ideas from the passage that you can reflect on from time to time during the day. With the wide variety of different styles of Bible reading plans available today, it is surprising how much of the Bible you can cover in this way. Some notes major on topics, using different Bible passages each day to help you focus on a particular theme or set of concerns, while others take a whole year to look at specific Bible passages – the life of Jesus, or the life and letters of Paul, for example. Yet others take you consecutively through extended, though not necessarily related passages of Scripture. So you need to know not only how much time you have available, but what kind of angle you would like to follow at any given moment. Suppose, however, that you have longer than this. You have an hour's journey by commuter train into the centre of a large city every day – and instead of passing the time wrestling with over-sized newspapers to the annoyance of your fellow passengers, you decide to do some Bible study. This period of time would certainly give you scope for a more intensive study of particular Bible books. Not only would you have time to read God's Word in a more leisurely way, but you would be able to reflect on it quite extensively. Here, one of the many simple commentaries or Bible handbooks could give you invaluable help – as well as the daily study notes. Of course you would not want to carry large volumes in your case, but even quite a comprehensive well-designed book is a good deal easier to control than that old newspaper!

Not everyone rides to work either by bus or train every day. Some go out by car, and others stay at home either because that is where they work, or because they have no work. Either way, you need not miss out on regular Bible reading. I have often used a cassette tape of Bible books while driving in the car, listening for ten minutes and then reflecting on it. In theory, I tell myself that it should make me a better driver if I'm reacting to other traffic on the road from God's perspective! The same device can be very useful too for the hard-pressed parent, looking after a home and small children, who just cannot find even five minutes in the day to sit and read books. But you can listen while you're cleaning the carpets, changing the baby, doing the laundry or whatever. These various possibilities must suit the lifestyle of most of us, so far as daily Bible reading is concerned. But if you were asked to go and speak to your church youth group on a particular passage, you would not (I hope) try and prepare for it either in short ten-minute bursts before you catch the bus, or in the monotonous environment of the daily commuter journey – and certainly not while driving the car! You would need to take time out one evening or weekend, so that you could concentrate on it for a while. After all, if you have not given the Bible passage *your* undivided attention, why should you expect your hearers to give you *theirs*?

These circumstances probably cover 95 per cent of the time most of us would give to Bible reading and study. Some are far more dedicated than that. I remember someone once telling me that his resolution on New Year's Day was to get through the whole Bible in a year – not just reading it, but working through commentaries, handbooks, and other aids to understanding, then thinking about it all and finally producing his own written notes on every chapter. I was more than surprised that he was still at it by Easter – and absolutely bowled over when he coolly informed me the next Christmas that he had not only achieved his objective, but had also taught himself New Testament Greek into the bargain! If you are the sort of person who can do that, then you probably don't need a book like this to tell you how. But most of us (including me) are made of softer stuff.

As well as developing different strategies in relation to the occasion and purpose for which you read the Bible, it can also be helpful to use different translations from time to time. If most of your Bible reading is of the ten-minutes-before-I-catch-the-bus variety (or, just as popular, two-minutes-before-I-fall-asleep-at-night), then you won't want to be wrestling with versions like the NRSV or NIV, which try and preserve something of the constructions and words of the original Hebrew and Greek texts. On the other hand, if your church youth group is in the habit of asking particularly complex questions, you might well find it worthwhile to look at a few knowledgeable commentaries, most of which tend to be based on versions like these. But it is important not to become a Bible snob, and to imagine that because some 'educated' writers prefer English versions that use refined and traditional theological words, they are somehow 'nearer the truth'. The fact is they are not. One of the criticisms levelled at the Good News Bible when it first came out was that it had degraded the Bible by using the sort of language you would find in tabloid newspapers. This was true, of course – but if the mark of a good translation is to produce literature that in English will make the same impact as it did in its original setting, then the character of the GNB's language ought to have been reason for high praise, not criticism. For the Greek of the New Testament writers did not bear much relation either to the up-market and intellectual writings of the Greek philosophers and historians, nor to the theological jargon developed by western Christians, and itself based on the very same Greek philosophical writings from which the New Testament was so different! The Greek of the New Testament was a written version of the language as it was spoken by ordinary people in the streets and homes of the first century Roman empire. Some of them were very ordinary: when Paul wrote to the church in the Greek city of Corinth, he observed that 'few of you were wise or powerful or of high social standing' (1 Corinthians 1:26). One or two were, of course, but they tended to be richer merchants and politicians, not professional academics and writers. Inasmuch as it is possible to make the same impact in today's world as the New Testament documents first made in theirs, there is no doubt that versions such as the Good News Bible or the Contemporary English Version are the ones most likely to do so, rather than more literalistic translations such as the NIV or NRSV.

The creative possibilities for understanding the Bible naturally increase in proportion to the amount of time you are prepared to give to it. In the very first chapter of this book, I commended the practice of reading complete books of the Bible through at one sitting, and I repeat that advice here. But what should we then do in order to understand as fully as possible what we read? Martin Luther described his own procedure like this: 'First I shake the whole tree, that the ripe fruit might fall. Then I climb the tree and shake each limb, and then each branch and then each twig, and then I look under each leaf.' He spent long days for many years just reading and thinking about the Bible. Few of us today have the time for that. But it is still worthwhile to try and structure our thinking on any given passage, in order to get the most out of it. I find it helpful to think of it in three ways, summed up in the three words Comprehension – Explanation – Application.

# Comprehension

The question to ask here is a very simple one: what does this passage actually say? You might think this hardly requires much thought, for presumably the Bible says what it means, just like any other book. But do we always allow it the freedom to mean what it says? Or do we make the unspoken assumption that our own way of life and church organisation are already in line with 'what the Bible says'? If we do, we can unwittingly defuse it so that it comes to us not as an explosive word from God speaking to us and challenging our own situation, but as a tame and domesticated supplement to our own thinking. You would be surprised how often Christians can assume that their own lifestyle and church traditions are 'biblical', when in fact they are no such thing. A historical example of this would be in South Africa, which for generations was one of the most religious countries in the world. The Dutch Reformed Church arrived there with the very first white settlers in 1652, and faith was always important to the Afrikaner population. As long ago as 1857, however, this church insisted that black and white Christians must not be allowed to worship together, and in due course the perception that separation between races was the will of God led to the emergence of the political system of apartheid in the mid–twentieth century. This led to untold misery for the majority of South Africa's people (who were not Afrikaners), and created significant tensions between the Dutch Reformed Church and other Christian bodies, who found no such thing anywhere in the Bible. It was not until 1986 that this church changed its stance and realised what other Christians had known all along, that (in the words of their own official statement), 'the application of apartheid ... cannot be accepted on Christian ethical grounds, since it conflicts with the principle of neighbourly love and righteousness'.

That is a particularly striking example of how people who love the Bible can sometimes read it without realising what the words are actually saying. But we also need to ask further questions about the Bible, in order to be quite clear about what it is saying. We need to reflect on some of the matters raised in earlier chapters here, and with any particular passage ask, for example, what is its historical context? Why was it written? What form does it have: is it poetry, or history, or fiction, or law, or letters, or what? And in that context, how am I meant to understand the actual words that are used? Obviously, for many of these questions you will need to take the advice of others, and this is where Bible handbooks in particular come into their own. For they help to answer questions like this, while not giving the kind of detailed explanation of individual sentences and phrases that you would find in a commentary.

## Explanation

Once we have clarified for ourselves what the words are *saying*, there is a further obvious question: what does this passage mean? What did it mean to the person who first wrote it, and more particularly, how would it speak to the people who first read it? What is its main point? What is it really saying? Not every passage of the Bible will yield very much in answer to questions like this. Many of the psalms, for example, really require no further explanation of this sort. They are hymns of praise, or prayers of various kinds, and they demand not more intellectual investigation, but an emotional response. The same thing is true of much of the teaching of Jesus.

But there are Bible passages whose significance can only be fully drawn out in this way. In 1 Corinthians 8, for example, Paul deals with the question of whether Christians should eat meat previously offered to idols. To the overwhelming majority of modern readers of Paul, that is simply a non-question – certainly in Western cultures - though in some parts of the world it would still be a living issue today. Yet it was of great consequence in Corinth, for there were no regular butchers' shops in an ancient city. The likelihood is that in Corinth some meat would be available within the Jewish community – but that was the last place that Gentile Christians would have been welcomed as shoppers. Their only realistic option therefore would be to buy and eat meat that had been offered to the traditional Greek and Roman deities, or go without meat entirely. What should they do? They had given up the worship of those very same gods in order to become Christians, and so the last thing they wanted was to appear to be giving credence to a form of worship that they had already rejected. Some of them felt it was not really important, for if these idols had no true existence anyway, then they could hardly have an effect on the quality of meat! Others were not so sure, and were not prepared to take the risk. In dealing with this question Paul recognised the reality of the predicament in which his Christian friends found themselves, and answered accordingly. From our standpoint today, we might wonder why Paul didn't advise them to become vegetarians, but he dealt with the issues as they were, and at the time this was not one of them.

Similar matters arise at other points in Paul's writings. Galatians, for example, is one of the central letters for understanding Paul's thinking. Yet the major question to which it addresses itself is this: should a person go out and get circumcised in order to be a good Christian? Very few of today's Christians will ever have asked that question. For a woman it would make absolutely no sense at all – but neither is it a burning religious issue for male Christians nowadays. The fact is that, like the business of food offered to idols, the whole matter of observing rules and regulations related to Judaism and the Old Testament – so crucially important in the first century AD – is totally irrelevant to the everyday lifestyle of just about all of today's Christians. But in order to appreciate what *is* relevant, we need to have some idea of why the Bible writers wrote and spoke as they did. In spite of the fact that they seem so remote, both the examples I have quoted here have clear meaning and value for us today. For in his discussion of the issue of circumcision in Galatians, Paul presents a wide-ranging consideration of the nature of Christian freedom. If we are free from the need to keep lots of rules in order to be good Christians, what does that mean in terms of living the Christian life? In the heat of that debate, Paul comes up with one of the most quotable quotes in the whole of his writings (Galatians 3:28). The same is true in 1 Corinthians 8, where in answer to the specific question Paul takes a line not unlike that of Jesus: people and their feelings, he says, are far more important to God than principles and ideas. That discussion also can provide some insights that are definitely relevant to the life of the church today. But in order to see more clearly what these insights are, and exactly how they might relate to the modern scene, we must go a stage further.

## Application

This is the point at which there can be a true interaction between ourselves and the Bible. In endeavouring to open our minds so that the Bible can speak to us, we must be prepared to speak to it. What are the issues that concern us today, and what is God saying to us about them? Here we need to be prepared to use our imagination. To some, that will seem a risky business. But it is an integral part of any true interaction between ourselves and our Bible. This is what delivers us from being only experts in ancient history. It is also the point at which we can most clearly perceive the meaning of Jesus' promise that the Holy Spirit will lead his followers into all the truth. For it is the Spirit who shows us what God is doing in our world today, and gives us insights into God's will and its challenge for our own lives.

There is always the possibility that individuals will go off at a tangent here, and develop subjective and speculative interpretations of the Bible. This is what happened in the very earliest centuries of the church's life, when as a result of the activities of extremist fringe groups like the Gnostics and others, the mainstream church evolved an elaborate pattern of controls to keep everyone in step, and ensure that the official line would be followed. Some are afraid that sections of the church today are in danger of repeating the same mistakes. It is not uncommon to hear it claimed that, by giving a place to the direct guidance of the Holy Spirit, the charismatic renewal movement has effectively undermined the authority of Scripture as being in some special way the word of God. This is a valid question, and needs to be taken seriously. Paul himself advised the Christians at Thessalonica to 'Put all things to the test' (1 Thessalonians 5:21), and discernment is one of the gifts of the Spirit, 'the ability to tell the difference between gifts that come from the Spirit and those that do not' (1 Corinthians 12:10). Two things need to be said here. To begin with, we must all remember that when we come to the Bible today we are not the first people in history to do so. For the whole of the church's long existence, men and women have studied the Bible and sought to discern through it what God is saying. In the process, a number of milestones and signposts have been set up along the way, encapsulated for the most part in the great historic creeds of the church. I have no doubt in my own mind that these creeds capture the essence of Christian belief as it is found in the Bible. They do not of course use Bible language to do so, and in some respects they go beyond what is literally stated in the Bible, though not further than what can reasonably be inferred from it. For all these reasons, the creeds are now in many respects deficient and unserviceable, mostly because much of their language, and the philosophical assumptions which they embody, are all but meaningless to people today. A strong case can be made out to support the view that the creeds need to be updated and rewritten as a matter of some urgency. A creed for today *should* surely look different from a creed for the fourth or fifth-century Roman world! Notwithstanding that, the statements they make on such topics as they cover do reflect what we find in the New Testament. We can therefore expect that what Gods says to us through the Bible today will not materially contradict what previous generations of Christians have believed through the centuries, and what has come to us as the historic Christian faith.

At the same time, it is hardly possible to deny that much Western Christianity, especially in the last hundred years, has not shown much evidence of the same dynamic quality of spiritual experience that was so much a part of church life in those early days. The New Testament itself assumes that God can and does speak in direct ways to us through the work of the Spirit: what else can 'prophecy' possibly be? One of the ancient endings to Mark's Gospel paints a picture of Christians experiencing in a very direct way the intervention of God in their lives (Mark 16:14–20). This paragraph was almost certainly not a part of what Mark actually wrote, but was added at some later date to round off the somewhat abrupt ending of his Gospel. But, for that very reason, we can be quite sure that it reflects the actual experience of the church at that time, and not some idealistic and romantic notion that never came to pass. Other leading lights of the early church also mention direct enlightenment through the work of the Spirit as part and parcel of everyday Christian experience – including such theological giants as Justin Martyr, Irenaeus, Tertullian, Novatian, Ambrose and Augustine. Martin Luther was also fully aware of the fact that while the great creeds give us a framework within which to interpret scripture, it requires the Spirit to address us directly in such a way that the words can take on a new meaning for our own context. Writing of prophecy, he commented that 'one may prophesy new things, though not things going beyond the bounds of faith'.

It is a mark of how secular even Christian thinkers can become that so many should want to play down the direct application of Scripture to the lives of Christians by the work of the Spirit. We have not become 'secular' in the sense of not believing in God, of course, but the God we feel most happy to believe in is often a typical God of the Enlightenment, who never surprises us and always does things that can be apprehended and controlled by human reason. As a result, Bible reading and Bible study become a dry and essentially intellectual procedure, filling heads with facts but rarely changing lives and certainly powerless to challenge effectively the world-view or structures of society. When we accept unthinkingly what others tell us about the Bible, we can easily slip into spiritual stagnation. But when we engage in a genuine interaction with the message of the Bible, and the living Word who stands behind it, that is a step along the road to spiritual growth. For when we expose ourselves directly to Scripture, God can and often does speak to us in new and creative ways. That is why Christians read the Bible: for the Word of God to be lifted from the pages of the book, and written in our lives so that we might worship and serve God the more effectively. God's people, informed by God's Word and motivated by God's Spirit is a winning combination, with the potential to engender a far-reaching renewal of both the church and the world.